Intermediate

Listening In & Speaking Out

Gary James
Charles G. Whitley
Sharon Bode

Longman
New York

LISTENING IN AND SPEAKING OUT
INTERMEDIATE

First printing 1980

Sponsoring Editor: Larry Anger
Project Editor: Karen Davy

Illustrations and Cover Design: Frederick Charles Ltd.
Design: Nilda Scherer

ISBN 0-582-79735-7

Longman
95 Church Street
White Plains, NY 10601

Distributed in the United Kingdom by Longman Group Ltd., Longman House, Burnt Mill, Harlow, Essex CM20 2JE, England, and by associated companies, branches and representatives throughout the world.

13 14 15 16 17 18 19 20-CRS-97 96 95 94 93

To the teachers who taught us the most:

RUTH CRYMES

INA MILLER

TED PLAISTER

and

To the students of the Kyoto YMCA English School

Acknowledgements

Over the years countless people have been involved in assisting us to bring these materials to their present form. We gratefully acknowledge their help and express our appreciation to:

Bette Matthews, who is the marvelous fourth voice in the discussions;
the entire Kyoto YMCA English School teaching staff, especially Kiyo Inagaki and Ray Mori, for their splendid support;
the administration of the Kyoto YMCA English School, including Yoshiyuki Kuroda, Shinichi Mitani, Yoshihiro Sakai, Taiichi Takaya and Seisuke Ue, for their faith in our efforts;
the office staff of the Kyoto YMCA English School, especially Toshiko Fujiwara, Takako Hata Itahara and Machiko Morimoto, for their devoted labors;
Akira Ogawa of Sangyo Daigaku and Katsumi Ige and his staff of Honolulu Community College, for their fine technical assistance in recording the materials;
Yutaka Akimaru and Tadashi Inoue, who made it possible to get earlier versions of the materials duplicated;
Susie Young and Robert Dilley of the American Language Institute, University of Southern California, for their willing assistance in duplicating tapes;
Al Hoel and Sharyn Klafehn, for their belief in the materials and their encouragement;
Clara Iwata, Kathy Langaman, Adela Rhoades and Arlene Yano of Honolulu Community College and Evangeline Colbero and Eleanor Curry of Chaminade University of Honolulu, for their excellent typing;
Bill Wiley and Lou Willand of Honolulu Community College and Eleanor Frierson of Chaminade University of Honolulu, for providing an academic atmosphere that has allowed these materials to flourish;
and Karen Davy and Larry Anger of Longman Inc. for their interest and editorial assistance.

Contents

Introduction

LISTENING IN AND SPEAKING OUT focuses on spontaneous spoken English with the aim of bridging the gap between "classroom English" and the English that students are likely to encounter on their own. The activities in the Student's Book are based on two kinds of recordings. The first is an unscripted Monolog which lasts approximately one minute. The second recording is an unrehearsed, spontaneous Discussion in which four native speakers exchange candid opinions about a particular topic. A recorded Discussion lasts about a minute and a half.

The recordings were made by four native speakers of English who come from various regions of the United States. They are good friends, which is illustrated by the language they use with each other. Three of the four speakers are the authors of this material: Sharon Bode, Gary James and Charles G. Whitley; the fourth person is Bette Matthews.

The skill of understanding English spoken at normal speed can be acquired only through practice in listening to *English spoken at normal speed*. Contrary to language heard in most recorded materials, the ordinary phenomena of spoken English (the English that is spoken in real conversations) are represented in LISTENING IN AND SPEAKING OUT. The listener will sometimes hear very rapid speech, and at other times somewhat slower varieties of delivery. The listener will hear interruptions, unfinished sentences, awkward or "incorrect" grammatical constructions, people talking simultaneously, ellipsis, strange logic and a wide range of emotional and intellectual "voices."

Besides developing listening comprehension skills by exposing students to informal spoken language, the aims of the LISO materials are: 1) to provide opportunities for students to talk; 2) to provide a classroom environment that is student- rather than teacher-centered; 3) to provide students with the confidence, motivation and ideas for on-going self-teaching.

DESCRIPTION OF THE ACTIVITIES AND SUGGESTIONS FOR THEIR USE

Although LISTENING IN AND SPEAKING OUT, INTERMEDIATE was written to be used as the primary text in a listening comprehension class, it can also be used as a supplementary text. It is not necessary to start with Unit One and go through the material in order; because the recorded material is totally unscripted, there is no vocabulary or structure control.

Getting Set. A dictated introduction to the recorded Monolog. This activity consists of four sentences that tell something about the subject of the recorded Monolog. It was written to be used before the students go over the vocabulary items and before they hear the recorded Monolog for the first time (even though it may contain some of the vocabulary items found in the Monolog).

Teachers do dictation practice in many different ways. The following is a suggested procedure. Of course, teachers can use any method they feel is appropriate for their students.

To prepare for dictation, the teacher writes the number one on the board. The teacher draws the same number of blank spaces as there are words in the line to be dictated. Depending on the level of the class, the teacher fills in one or more blanks with a word or words from the line to be dictated. Dictation can be as easy or as difficult as the teacher chooses.

The teacher then does the same thing on the board for lines 2, 3 and 4. The teacher's preparation for dictation practice is now completed, and the students copy what is written on the board. The teacher then tells the class to listen to each line. The teacher turns on the cassette recorder and plays each line from one to four times, depending on the level of the students, while the class listens. After each line has been played as many times as necessary, the teacher tells the class to write the line. While they are writing, the teacher quickly moves around the class looking at the students' work. The teacher can circle words that are incorrect and draw blank lines to indicate missing words. The teacher can then play the line again and have the class try to complete the sentence.

After each line has been played, if the students are sitting in small groups, the teacher can tell them to quickly compare and discuss their work. If the students are sitting together as a class, the teacher can simply move on to the second line of the dictation.

After all four lines have been written by the students, the teacher plays the entire dictation straight through. Dictation practice can be checked in many different ways. The following is a suggested procedure:

The teacher tells four students to each write one line of the dictated introduction on the board. This is checked and discussed, and students correct their papers. The teacher then tells the class to write the corrected introduction in their books. If the teacher wants, he or she can collect the corrected dictations in order to comment on the students' work. The text for **Getting Set** can be found in the Answer Key.

Tuning In. Vocabulary items likely to be unfamiliar to intermediate-level students. These should be reviewed in class before the students hear the Monolog or Discussion. It is helpful to provide examples of the new words in sentences and/or have students create their own sentences. Sometimes the meaning of a new word or expression will not be fully understood until after the students hear it used in the Monolog or Discussion. For lower-level students, the tape can be stopped frequently to focus on the new vocabulary in context.

Summing Up. Five statements that summarize the Monolog or the Discussion. The statements are in a multiple-choice format and were written as an exercise to aid comprehension and not as a test.

Before listening to the Monolog or the Discussion, read the multiple-choice activity together. The class either reads through the exercise silently or the teacher reads it through while the class listens and follows along. Reading the statements first should help students to focus on essential information as they listen. Then have students close their books while they listen to the recording. Play the Monolog or the Discussion as many times as necessary until students feel that they have grasped the general content. Finally, ask the students to do the comprehension exercise. It can be quickly checked and discussed either in small groups or by the whole class. The correct responses for **Summing Up** can be found in the Answer Key.

Retelling. Students give their own version of the Monolog or Discussion. This activity can be done orally or as written work. If the teacher feels students are able, they can paraphrase what they have heard without the help of the phrases given in the Student's Book.

As an oral activity, students can take turns retelling the Monolog or Discussion to the whole class or they can work in pairs or small groups. If necessary, one person can follow the Transcript to help the others. For pairs or small groups, the teacher circulates around the class, providing assistance when requested. The teacher should refrain from correcting students' grammar or pronunciation during the retelling in order to encourage them to express the ideas they heard and to develop their confidence in speaking.

Filling In. A cloze activity based on the transcript of the recorded material. Students are to fill in the blanks with the words they hear on the cassette. By now they have listened to the recordings several times and should be familiar enough with the context to be able to focus on specific words.

The cloze activity can be used as a test. The following is a suggested procedure for the **Filling In** exercise: The teacher should play the Monolog or Discussion straight through while students read along as they listen. Then the cassette is rewound and played until just past the first blank; using the instant stop or pause button, students are allowed enough time to write the word. For more advanced students, the tape can be stopped after longer segments of speech. Before the students check their answers, the entire text should be played through again. They can check their own exercises by comparing their answers with the text in the Tapescript. Have them circle their errors without writing the correct forms in the blanks. Then play the recording again and ask students to correct their errors as they listen. They can check their exercises again with the Tapescript or review the correct forms orally with the class.

Pairing Up. A dialog activity to be done in pairs. The two topics are related to the Monolog, Discussion or the discussion topics found in **Speaking Out**. Before beginning the activity, read through the parts for **A** and **B** with the whole class to be sure that everyone understands the conversation. You want students to feel comfortable with their parts so that they do not have to *read* the lines as they converse. Students should sit in pairs; one student is **A** and the other is **B**. As soon as **A** has asked the first question, **B** should silently read the suggested responses, then choose one or give his or her own answer. When students have finished the activity, they should switch parts and do it again. The correct forms for **A**'s questions are given in the Answer Key.

Drawing Out. Five statements about the four speakers in the Discussion. The information in these statements may or may not be reasonably inferred from what was said (or not said) in the Discussion. This exercise is to be used as a speaking activity and encourages students not only to understand the information exchanged in the Discussion, but also motivates them to use their imagination and to voice and defend their own opinions. Divide the class into five groups and assign one statement to each group. Ask them to discuss the statement among themselves, then to appoint a member to present the group's conclusion to the whole class. The answers to **Drawing Out** are given in the Answer Key.

Speaking Out. Discussion topics to talk or write about. By listening to the recorded Monologs and Discussions and doing the various preceding exercises, the students develop communication skills in a very fundamental way. As their perception and understanding of how native speakers of English actually talk to each other increase, their own ability to communicate increases also. The discussion topics allow students to interact in groups or pairs and to apply the vocabulary, expressions and "conversational tools" they have focused on in LISTENING IN AND SPEAKING OUT.

The following is a suggested procedure for the classroom management of this activity: Students form small groups of three or four people each. Each group decides on a topic of interest to all the members. The process itself of choosing a topic can become an interesting speaking activity. For homework, students write a short paragraph or composition, stating their ideas on the topic. The writing exercise should help them organize their ideas for the group discussion. When the class meets again, students in each group read each other's papers to become familiar with the other members' ideas. This will often help to "break the ice." Having each person write something will also encourage everyone in the group to participate in the discussion. As in the **Retelling** activity, the teacher can listen to the groups by circulating around the class, but it is important not to interrupt students to correct their speech. Students should feel that this activity is an opportunity for them to converse freely in English, as well as a chance to get to know the other people in their group.

Answer Key. The correct responses for **Getting Set, Summing Up, Pairing Up** and **Drawing Out**.

Tapescript. A complete transcription of the recorded Monologs and Discussions, with the language written exactly as it was spoken.

UNIT ONE
THE BIRTHDAY PARTY
Monolog

Getting Set

Listen to the recording, and write the sentences of the introduction in the lines below.

1. ______________________________ (7 words)

2. ______________________________ (6 words)

3. ______________________________ (7 words)

4. ______________________________ (6 words)

Tuning In

Check to see if you know the meanings of these words from the monolog.

1. *to know better than to:* to know enough not to
2. *to head for (a place)*: to go in the direction of (a place)
3. *desperate:* almost without hope
4. *to join in:* to begin to participate in an event that has already begun
5. *to upset (someone or something)*: to disturb

Summing Up

Read these five statements about the monolog. Listen to the recording as many times as you like. Then choose the best answer for each of the statements, and write the letter in the space.

1. Chuck doesn't like birthday parties ______.
   a. that are noisy
   b. that are expensive
   c. for himself
   d. for others

2. One year Chuck's friends had ______ party for him.
   a. a surprise
   b. a beach
   c. a formal
   d. an office

3. Chuck's friends were ______ in his apartment when he got home from school.
   a. preparing dinner
   b. watching television
   c. studying
   d. hiding

4. Chuck ______ and spoiled the surprise.
   a. went to the kitchen to get some water
   b. went to the bathroom to wash his hands
   c. got angry with his roommate
   d. got angry with his friends

5. The person behind the shower curtain started singing because ______.
   a. she wanted Chuck to know she was there
   b. she didn't know Chuck was there
   c. Chuck liked her voice
   d. she was happy

Retelling

Tell the story in your own words. You may use the sentences below as a guide.

Chuck likes birthday parties when ______________________________

______________________________, but ______________________________

______________________________.

Once, some friends of his ______________________________

______________________________.

Chuck got home from school at about 3:30, and ______________________________

______________________________.

Then he heard ______________________________

______________________________. People ______________________________

______________________________.

Filling In

Listen to the recording, and fill in the blanks. You may listen to the monolog as many times as you need to.

If you know me very well, you know I don't like birthday parties. At least, I don't ________ (1) birthday parties given for, uh, ________ (2). I enjoy them when ________ (3) for other people, but ________ (4) they're for me, I ________ (5) don't like them.

I ________ (6) one birthday party some ________ (7) of mine had for ________ (8) when I was a ________ (9) at the university. Of ________ (10), I, uh, had told my ________ (11) that I didn't want ________ (12) party and I made ________ (13) promise he wouldn't do ________ (14). He agreed and I ________ (15) known better than to ________ (16) him.

On the day ________ (17) my birthday, we got ________ (18) from school at about, oh, ________ (19) don't know, three or three-thirty. ________ (20) went inside and as ________ (21) I headed for the ________ (22). I went inside and ________ (23) to close the door ________ (24) suddenly from behind the ________ (25) curtain, a kind of ________ (26)-sounding female voice started ________ (27), "Happy birthday to you, ________ (28) birthday to you."

And ________ (29) from all over the ________ (30), people joined in. There ________ (31) about fifteen people hiding ________ (32) in the apartment. They ________ (33) gotten my roommate's key ________ (34) gone in earlier. They ________ (35) all planned to come ________ (36) of hiding just at ________ (37) same time while singing. ________ (38) guess I really upset ________ (39) plans by going in ________ (40) to wash my hands.

GIVING GIFTS

Discussion

Work with another student. One of you will be **A,** and the other will be **B.** When you finish the activity, change parts and repeat it. Student **B** may answer with one of the choices, or s/he may provide his/her own response.

Giving Gifts

STUDENT A: (Ask B if s/he likes to give gifts.)

____?

STUDENT B: 1. Yes. I like to.
2. No. I don't really like to.

3. ____.

STUDENT A: (Ask B what kind of gifts s/he likes to give.)

____?

STUDENT B: 1. Almost anything.
2. Things that are useful.

3. ____.

STUDENT A: (Ask B if s/he likes to give gifts any time.)

____?

STUDENT B: 1. Yes. Not just on holidays and birthdays.
2. No. Just at certain times.

3. ____.

Money and Happiness

STUDENT A: (Ask B if happiness depends on money.)

____?

STUDENT B: 1. Yes. I guess for me it does.
2. No. For me they're not related.

3. ____.

STUDENT A: (Ask B how long s/he's felt that way.)

____?

STUDENT B: 1. As far back as I can remember.
2. I've only felt that way lately.

3. ____.

STUDENT A: (Ask B if money could help make someone a better person.)

____?

STUDENT B: 1. Sure. You could do a lot to help other people.
2. No. I doubt that it could at all.

3. ____.

Now change parts, and repeat the activity.

Tuning In

Check to see if you know the meanings of these words from the discussion.

1. *gum* : a candy to chew—not to eat
2. *to pick up* (*something*) : to buy
3. *formalistic:* traditional
4. . . . *and stuff* : (informal) "and other things like that"

Read these statements about the discussion. Listen to the recording as many times as you like. Then choose the best answer for each of the statements, and write the letter in the space.

1. Chuck and Sharon like to give gifts ________.
   a. at appropriate times
   b. at special times
   c. when they feel they should
   d. when they feel like it
2. Everyone except Sharon thought gum was ________ gift.
   a. an appropriate
   b. a memorable
   c. a required
   d. a funny
3. Sharon likes to buy small things that people ________.
   a. might usually buy for themselves
   b. might not buy for themselves
   c. might not have enough money to buy
   d. might not really want
4. Gary likes to give gifts ________.
   a. at appropriate times
   b. at unexpected times
   c. that are expensive
   d. that are inexpensive
5. Gary believes ________ is important for remembering when to give gifts.
   a. a calendar
   b. a special form
   c. a system of recording
   d. a system of choosing

Retelling

Retell the discussion in your own words. You may use the sentences below as a guide.

The people are talking about ____.

The first man (Chuck) ____.

One woman (Sharon) likes to give small gifts. For example, she ____________________

____.

The man who likes to give gifts (Gary) gives them ____________________

____. Maybe it's easy for

him to give gifts because ____

______________________________. One of the women (Sharon) has trouble

remembering ____.

Drawing Out

Read the statements below. Listen to the discussion, and think about what the speakers are saying. Then decide if each statement is *possible* or *not probable* because of the information in the discussion. Find some evidence to support your answer.

1. Bette might have laughed at Sharon because she thought gum was a cheap gift.
2. Gary would probably give more expensive gifts than the other three people in the discussion.
3. Gary probably forgets many things when he goes shopping.
4. Chuck might buy candy bars or bubble gum to give as gifts.
5. Sharon is probably embarrassed because she can't remember dates.

Filling In

Listen to the recording, and fill in the blanks. You may listen to the discussion as many times as you need to.

CHUCK: You know, I really don't like having to give gifts on like Christmases and birthdays and stuff, but I like giving gifts very much on times when I just feel like doing it.

SHARON: I do too. And ________ (1) give gifts to a ________ (2) of people that way. ________ (3), uh, maybe I like giving ________ (4) at Christmas too, but ________ (5) so much as an ________ (6). When I was little, ________ (7) did.

BETTE: Well, what kind ________ (8) gifts do you like ________ (9) give, Sharon?

SHARON: Almost anything. ________ (10) mean, sometimes, uh, gum or ________ (11) or . . . (*laughter*)

GARY: You give gum?

BETTE: You really go all out, don't you? (*laughter*)

SHARON: Well, no, but what I mean is, you know, ________ (12) I walk by a ________ (13) and I see a ________ (14) of foreign cigarettes and ________ (15) know somebody likes them ________ (16) doesn't usually buy them ________ (17) themselves, I, you know, ________ (18) might pick up a ________ (19) and give them to somebody.

CHUCK: Yeah, that's nice.

GARY: When do you give . . .

BETTE: How about you, Gary?

GARY: When you . . . when do you . . . sorry . . . when do you give ________ (20) of gum? (*laughter*)

SHARON: Well, just ________ (21), my mother's been here ________ (22) she likes to chew ________ (23) and I don't usually ________ (24) it, but when I ________ (25) it now, you know, ________ (26) might stop and just ________ (27) her a pack of ________ (28).

GARY: Mmm.

SHARON: Just for fun.

GARY: I like to give ________ (29).

SHARON: Yeah, I know you ________ (30).

BETTE: You want to give ________ (31) one? (*laughter*)

GARY: Well, it's not ________ (32) birthday, is it?

CHUCK: Do you . . . Gary, ________ (33) you like to give, ________ (34) you like giving gifts ________ (35) time or just at certain times?

GARY: Yeah, I was going to say, uh, it's ________ (36) Bette's birthday and I ________ (37) to give gifts at ________ (38) occasions. I differ with ________ (39) on that. At Christmas ________ (40) birthdays, anniversaries and things ________ (41) that, I like to ________ (42) gifts.

BETTE: You're rather formalistic, then?

GARY: Very much so that __________ 43.

SHARON: But I think you __________ 44 . . . much better memory than __________ 45 rest of us. I __________ 46 one reason I like __________ 47 give gifts all the __________ 48 is 'cause I re-, never __________ 49 the appropriate times.

GARY: Well, you __________ 50 to have a system of re-, __________ 51.

CHUCK: Yeah, I have that __________ 52 also.

SHARON: Yeah. Yeah, I, 'cause __________ have so many brothers __________ sisters and other people, __________ 55 don't remember birthdays and __________ 56.

CHUCK: You can write it __________ 57.

Speaking Out

Read the discussion suggestions below, and choose one to talk or write about.

1. GIVING GIFTS: Do you enjoy giving gifts? What kinds of gifts do you like to give? What are the traditional times for gift-giving in your country?
2. MONEY AND HAPPINESS: Some people believe that money and happiness are closely related. Do you believe this? What things make you happy?
3. BIRTHDAYS: Do you like to celebrate your birthday? Your friends' birthdays? How do you celebrate?

UNIT TWO
THE PHONE CALL
Monolog

Getting Set

Listen to the recording, and write the sentences of the introduction in the lines below.

1. ____ (9 words)
2. ____ (6 words)
3. ____ (10 words)
4. ____ (7 words)

Tuning In

Check to see if you know the meanings of these words from the monolog.

1. *kind of* (+ adjective): a little
2. *to take* (*so*) *long:* to spend a (very) long time

Read these five statements about the monolog. Listen to the recording as many times as you like. Then choose the best answer for each of the statements, and write the letter in the space.

1. Gary wanted to make a phone call at the airport, but all of the phones were ________.
   a. too far
   b. too noisy
   c. being used
   d. being repaired
2. Gary began to ________ the telephone conversation of an old man.
   a. break in on
   b. listen in on
   c. write down
   d. laugh about
3. The old man was ________ while talking on the phone.
   a. laughing and joking
   b. talking and writing
   c. sitting and smoking
   d. eating and drinking
4. Gary became impatient because ________.
   a. he had to buy a gift
   b. he had to buy his ticket
   c. he had to wait a long time
   d. he had to meet someone
5. The old man told Gary he was having ________ with his wife.
   a. dinner
   b. tea
   c. an argument
   d. a meeting

Retelling

Tell the story in your own words. You may use the sentences below as a guide.

While Gary was waiting for his flight, he had to ____________________

____________________, but ____________________.

While ____________________, he listened ____________________

____________________. Gary became impatient because ____________________

____________________. Finally, the old man ____________________

____________________ and he said ____________________

____________________.

Filling In

Listen to the recording, and fill in the blanks. You may listen to the monolog as many times as you need to.

Last time I was at a plane, uh, an airport, I, uh, was between planes and I had to make an important phone call and I looked around . . . all the phones that I could see were busy. So I waited in ______ (1) and waited and waited. ______ (2) finally, uh, the person who ______ (3) talking on the phone ______ (4) I was waiting for . . . ______ (5) to use, uh, I . . . I . . . I began ______ (6) listen to his conversation.

______ (7) was kind of funny ______ (8) he was an old ______ (9) and he was talking ______ (10) his wife and he ______ (11) talking about his trip. ______ (12) he said, uh, that he, uh, he ______ (13) having a good time ______ (14) he talked about the ______ (15) and he asked about ______ (16) weather back there. And ______ (17) the time he was ______ (18), uh, to his wife . . . I ______ (19) it was to his ______ (20), but while he was ______ (21) to his wife, he . . . he ______ (22) eating a sandwich and, uh, ______ (23) coffee.

And this went ______ (24) and on and on, ______ (25) I really was getting ______ (26) because this phone call ______ (27) had to make was ______ (28). And, uh, maybe

I waited ________ [29] . . . oh, ten, fifteen, twenty minutes. ________ [30] finally the guy hung ________ [31] and he turned around ________ [32] he . . . he had seen ________ [33] standing there, and he ________ [34], "Well, I'm sorry, uh, that ________ [35] took so long on ________ [36] phone, but I was ________ [37] dinner with my wife."

WAITING

Discussion

Work with another student. One of you will be **A,** and the other will be **B.** When you finish the activity, change parts and repeat it. Student **B** may answer with one of the choices, or s/he may provide his/her own response.

Waiting

STUDENT A: (Ask B if waiting a long time bothers him/her.)

______________________________?

STUDENT B: 1. Yeah. It bothers me a lot.
2. No. I don't mind so much.

3. ______________________________.

STUDENT A: (Ask B how s/he feels when s/he has to wait.)

______________________________?

STUDENT B: 1. I really get impatient because I don't like it.
2. I don't have any special feeling.

3. ______________________________.

STUDENT A: (Ask B if it helps to get impatient.)

______________________________?

STUDENT B: 1. I don't know, but it makes me feel better.
2. No. It just makes me feel worse.

3. ______________________________.

Using the Phone

STUDENT A: (Ask B if s/he uses the telephone often.)

______________________________?

STUDENT B: 1. Yeah. I do a lot.
2. No. Not really very much.

3. ______________________________.

STUDENT A: (Ask B what s/he usually uses the phone for.)

______________________________?

STUDENT B: 1. Usually just for important things.
2. I just like to talk to friends.

3. ______________________________.

STUDENT A: (Ask B if s/he talks a long time on the phone.)

______________________________?

STUDENT B: 1. Yeah. I really enjoy it.
2. No. I try to keep calls short.

3. ______________________________

Tuning In

Check to see if you know the meanings of these words from the discussion.

1. *disgusted:* feeling deeply negative
2. *How about* ______?: (Use these words to make a suggestion.)
3. *the very* (+ noun): exact

Summing Up

Read these statements about the discussion. Listen to the recording as many times as you like. Then choose the best answer for each of the statements, and write the letter in the space.

1. If Sharon knows someone will be late, she ______.
   a. is still bothered by waiting
   b. is happy to wait
   c. usually leaves without the person
   d. reads something
2. Bette felt ______ when her friend didn't wait in line to buy movie tickets.
   a. impatient
   b. relieved
   c. disgusted
   d. embarrassed
3. Chuck thinks getting impatient ______.
   a. makes his friends get angry
   b. doesn't make his friends get angry
   c. improves the situation
   d. doesn't improve the situation
4. Bette says that if a friend she's waiting for is late, she ______.
   a. complains a lot later
   b. wants to know why later
   c. leaves
   d. waits
5. ______ are the two people in the conversation who are most impatient while waiting.
   a. Bette and Chuck
   b. Gary and Sharon
   c. Chuck and Gary
   d. Chuck and Sharon

Retelling

Retell the discussion in your own words. You may use the sentences below as a guide.

The people are talking about ______________________________.

The first man (Gary) was disturbed because ______________________________

______________. The first woman (Sharon) also ______________________________

________________________, but the other man (Chuck) ________________

________________. The second woman (Bette) had a friend who ____________

____

________________. Sharon gets impatient when she ________________

________________________because ________________________________

________________. When someone Bette knows is always late, she ____________

____.

Drawing Out

Read the statements below. Listen to the discussion again, and think about what the speakers are saying. Then decide if each statement is *possible* or *not probable* because of the information in the discussion. Find some evidence to support your answer.

1. Sharon probably pushes buttons to close elevator doors.
2. Bette and Chuck might be willing to wait in line all night to buy good concert tickets.
3. Gary might have a good friend who is often late.
4. Chuck might prefer living in a country where people believe that it is very important to be on time.
5. Gary and Sharon might keep bus and train schedules in their wallets.

Filling In

Listen to the recording, and fill in the blanks. You may listen to the discussion as many times as you need to.

GARY: I really got disgusted this morning.

SHARON: Why, Gary?

GARY: Well, we ________ (1) waiting for a taxi ________ (2) come here and none ________ (3).

SHARON: Oh, I hate to ________ (4) like that, you know.

GARY: ________ (5) do too.

BETTE: Well, yeah, ________ (6) sometimes you . . . you . . . what can ________ (7) do about it, you ________ (8)?

SHARON: Well, I'd rather . . .

CHUCK: I don't mind waiting so much.

SHARON: Really? I'm . . . I'm a ________(9) impatient person when I'm ________(10) for people.

CHUCK: Really, Sharon?

SHARON: Yeah. Or ________(11) for things like taxis.

CHUCK: ________(12) about if you have ________(13) appointment with somebody and ________(14) a few minutes late? ________(15) that bother you very ________(16)?

SHARON: If I know they're ________(17) to be late, not ________(18) much, although inside I ________(19) feel, mmm, very, mmm, strange because ________(20) don't like to wait ________(21).

CHUCK: Really?

BETTE: You know, I used ________(22) have this friend ________(23) hated to wait in li— . . . in ________(24) and I think this ________(25) probably something cultural, but ________(26) we would go someplace ________(27) to a theater and ________(28) be a long line, ________(29) would run up to ________(30) very front, and just . . . just ________(31) in front of everybody ________(32) his tickets.

SHARON: Oh, I don't like that.

CHUCK: So you always got in very fast.

BETTE: Of course we did, but, you know, I . . . I . . .

SHARON: Weren't you embarrassed by that?

BETTE: I . . . yeees . . . yes.

SHARON: I . . . I don't know, you know, when I go home ________(33) school at night, I ________(34) home with Kathy. And ________(35) she talks to her ________(36) after class and I ________(37) get impatient waiting 'cause ________(38) miss the train if ________(39) doesn't hurry.

CHUCK: Well, that's ________(40) different . . . I can understand ________(41) impatient in that situation ______ (42) . . . you'd miss your train. ______ (43) if you're just sort ______ (44) waiting in line or ______ (45) in a bank or ______ (46) . . . I don't . . . I don't think it's . . . ______ (47) to get impatient.

GARY: How ______ (48) you feel when you ______ (49) for the same person ______ (50) that person's always late? ______ (51) and over and . . .

BETTE: I just leave without them.

SHARON: Really?

BETTE: (*laughter*) Yes.

GARY: But it doesn't help.

SHARON: Not much.

BETTE: Well . . .

CHUCK: No, but . . .

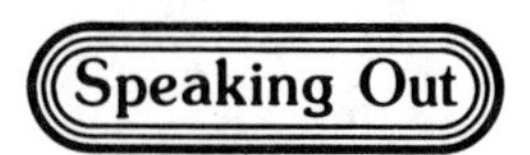

Read the discussion suggestions below, and choose one to talk or write about.

1. PATIENCE: What kinds of situations make you impatient? Why? Do you consider yourself a patient person or an impatient person? Why?
2. FEELING EMBARRASSED: Have you ever been embarrassed because of something a friend did? What was the situation? What happened?
3. IMPORTANCE OF TIME: Is being on time and following time schedules important to you? Why? Do your friends feel the same?

UNIT THREE
THE MOVIE DIRECTOR
Monolog

Getting Set

Listen to the recording, and write the sentences of the introduction in the lines below.

1. ______________________________ (7 words)
2. ______________________________ (7 words)
3. ______________________________ (10 words)
4. ______________________________ (9 words)

Check to see if you know the meanings of these words from the monolog.

1. *incomprehensible:* impossible to understand
2. *sets :* scene decorations
3. *elaborate:* fancy
4. *to figure out:* to understand completely

Summing Up

Read these statements about the monolog. Listen to the recording as many times as you like. Then choose the best answer for each of the statements, and write the letter in the space.

1. People usually ______ the movie director's English.
   a. praised c. understood
   b. copied d. didn't understand
2. The director ______ the assistant director about the lighting for one scene.
   a. wrote c. disagreed with
   b. telephoned d. agreed with
3. The assistant director thought the director said to ______ the set.
   a. find c. paint
   b. remove d. buy
4. The director really told the assistant director to ______ on the set.
   a. take visitors c. put more light
   b. not take visitors d. put less light
5. The assistant director ______ the director's pronunciation of the word *illuminate.*
   a. laughed at c. admired
   b. wrote down d. misunderstood

Retelling

Tell the story in your own words. You may use the sentences below as a guide.

The story is about a ____________ who had a problem with ____________
____________. Once when he was making a movie, his assistant and he disagreed about ____________.
The assistant thought that ____________
____________, but the director said ____________.
The next morning, ____________
____________.
The director had wanted the assistant to ____________, but instead, the assistant had ____________.

Filling In

Listen to the recording, and fill in the blanks. You may listen to the monolog as many times as you need to.

I heard a story about a movie director who was making a movie a few years ago. And this guy had ____(1) . . . problem with English. He'd . . . ____(2) speak but often people ____(3) understand what he ____(4) saying. He was almost ____(5).

Well, the movie company ____(6) spent lots and lots ____(7) money to make this ____(8). And the . . . and the, uh, sets ____(9) very expensive . . . hundreds and ____(10) of dollars. And there ____(11) this one scene in ____(12) movie that the assistant ____(13) had decided to film ____(14) almost total darkness for ____(15) special effect. And the, the ____(16), uh . . . movie director said, "No, no, ____(17) terrible. I don't like ____(18) at all."

And the ____(19) director said, "But it's ____(20), you know. It's very ____(21)."

And finally the director ________(22) the man down and ________(23) said, "Eliminate it! Just ________(24) it!"

Well, the sets ________(25) very elaborate, you know, ________(26) what can you do? ________(27), the next morning the ________(28) went to the movie ________(29) and he looked around ________(30) he didn't see the ________(31) at all. And it ________(32) such an expensive set ________(33) couldn't figure it out. ________(34) he went and found ________(35) assistant director and he ________(36), "Where is that set? ________(37) was a very expensive ________(38)."

And the assistant director ________(39), "Well, you told me ________(40) eliminate it."

And the ________(41) said, "No, you idiot. ________(42) didn't say, 'Eliminate it,' ________(43) said, 'Illuminate it!' "

Discussion

Pairing Up

Work with another student. One of you will be **A,** and the other will be **B.** When you finish the activity, change parts and repeat it. Student **B** may answer with one of the choices, or s/he may provide his/her own response.

Jobs

STUDENT A: (Ask B what kind of job s/he'd like to have.)

____?

STUDENT B:
1. I'd like to work as a/an ____________.
2. Just what I'm doing now.
3. ____.

STUDENT A: (Ask how important salary is.)

____?

STUDENT B:
1. It's really pretty important.
2. Not as important as personal satisfaction.
3. ____.

STUDENT A: (Ask B if s/he likes a lot of rules.)

____?

STUDENT B:
1. No. I like thinking for myself.
2. ________. So I don't have to make the decisions.
3. ____.

Using English

STUDENT A: (Ask B what his/her biggest problem in English is.)

____?

STUDENT B:
1. Understanding what people say.
2. Expressing what I want to say.
3. ____.

STUDENT A: (Ask B why s/he thinks it's a problem.)

____?

STUDENT B:
1. I need to spend more time with English speakers.
2. 'Cause I don't have enough confidence.
3. ____.

STUDENT A: (Ask B what his/her strongest point is.)

____?

STUDENT B: 1. Probably reading.
2. Maybe writing.
3. ______________________________.

Tuning In

Check to see if you know the meanings of these words from the discussion.

1. *spaced* : (slang) out of touch with the world
2. *essay:* a short piece of writing—not poetry or a short story

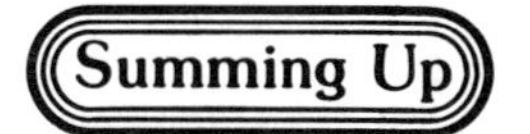

Summing Up

Read these statements about the discussion. Listen to the recording as many times as you like. Then choose the best answer for each of the statements, and write the letter in the space.

1. Chuck likes to do things that are ______.
   a. not serious
   b. not difficult
   c. new
   d. artistic
2. Sharon likes ______ very much.
   a. flying
   b. teaching
   c. painting
   d. acting
3. One thing Bette wants to be is ______.
   a. a space pilot
   b. a teacher
   c. an anthropologist
   d. a musician
4. Chuck and Sharon would both like to be ______.
   a. dancers
   b. mathematicians
   c. musicians
   d. writers
5. ______ has no ideas about other possible jobs.
   a. Bette
   b. Chuck
   c. Gary
   d. Sharon

Retelling

Retell the discussion in your own words. You may use the sentences below as a guide.

The first man (Gary) asked the other teachers ______________________________
______________________________. The other man (Chuck) said ______________________________
______________________________. The other teachers mentioned

several other possibilities, including ______________________________________

____. But Gary ____________

____.

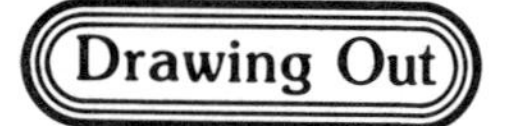

Read the statements below. Listen to the discussion, and think about what the speakers are saying. Then decide if each statement is *possible* or *not probable* because of the information in the discussion. Find some evidence to support your answer.

1. Bette probably likes classical music.
2. Sharon has probably had good experiences as a teacher.
3. Bette probably thinks Chuck doesn't like mathematics.
4. Gary probably knew before the discussion that Chuck wanted to be a space pilot.
5. Sharon might like to read about politics more than about fashion.

Filling In

Listen to the recording, and fill in the blanks. You may listen to the discussion as many times as you need to.

GARY: If you had to choose, what kind of job would you, uh, uh, do?

CHUCK: I'd like to be ______ (1) space pilot.

GARY: A space pilot!

SHARON: A space pilot?

GARY: Why?

BETTE: 'Cause he's ______ (2)! (*laughter*)

CHUCK: That's right.

GARY: No, seriously . . .

CHUCK: Because I think ______ (3) would really be ______ (4) and it's new . . .

GARY: You're really serious?

CHUCK: I ______ (5) am. Very serious. Yeah. That's true.

SHARON: Really? I never ______ (6) about it. I . . . I . . . mmm . . . I really like teaching.

BETTE: Just think of all that math you'd have to take.

GARY: ________ (7) like teaching, Sharon.

SHARON: Mmm, very ________ (8). But . . .

CHUCK: Well, of course, ________ (9) like teaching.

SHARON: But . . . I ________ (10) if I had to ________ (11) any kind of job, ________ (12) think teaching is really what I'd want to do.

CHUCK: But choose something besides teaching . . . what would you do?

GARY: Yeah, yeah. Choose something besides teaching.

SHARON: Mmm, ________ (13) I chose something besides ________ (14) . . .

BETTE: I'd be, uh, a violinist.

SHARON: Really?

BETTE: Or a ________ (15) pianist.

SHARON: Really?
BETTE: Yeah.
CHUCK: Really, Bette?
SHARON: Hmm.
CHUCK: Hmm.

GARY: The reason I asked ________ (16) because I just don't ________ (17) any idea of what ________ (18) would want to be.

CHUCK: Aren't ________ (19) things you'd like to ________ (20)? Oh, I can think of ________ (21) things just . . .

BETTE: Oh, a dancer too . . .
CHUCK: . . . very quickly that I'd like to be.
BETTE: I'd love to be a dancer.
SHARON: Hah!

CHUCK: I'd like to be ________ (22) anthropologist.

BETTE: Or an actor . . .
CHUCK: I'd like to be a writer.
BETTE: . . . uh, I mean an actress.
SHARON: Oh, that's what I'd like to do!
GARY: What?

SHARON: . . . you know, really. I would ________ (23) like to be a ________ (24).

CHUCK: What kind of things would you like to write?
GARY: Oh, that's hard work.
BETTE: A poet.
SHARON: Essays.
CHUCK: Essays?
SHARON: Mmm.
CHUCK: What kind of essays?

SHARON: I . . . I just like ________ (25) whole idea of writing ________ (26). You know, of . . . of really ________ (27) about something and then ________ (28) . . . that way. Although I . . . I ________ (29) also like to write ________ (30) stories.

CHUCK: I like doing ________ (31) things that haven't been ________ (32) before. That's why I'd ________ (33) to be a space ________ (34).

SHARON: Mmm.

GARY: That's been done before.

CHUCK: Well, yeah, mmm, ________ (35) time they do it though, it's different.

BETTE: Not to Venus.

CHUCK: That's ________ (36) or there's many places ________ (37) . . . yeah. Oh, I'd really like to ________ (38) it.

SHARON: Go ahead, Gary, think. ________ (39) would you like to ________ (40)?

GARY: Well, the reason why ________ (41) asked all of you ________ (42) because I have no ________ (43). I wanted to get ________ (44) opinions.

Speaking Out

Read the discussion suggestions below, and choose one to talk or write about.

1. JOBS: If you could choose any job, what kind of job would you choose? Why? In choosing a (permanent) job, what do you think is the most important thing: salary, personal happiness, company status, the feelings of your parents and/or friends, etc.?
2. EQUAL PAY: How do you feel about women and men doing the same kinds of jobs? Do you think they should be paid the same amount of money for the same work?
3. BEING INFLUENCED BY OTHERS: People who are well known, such as writers, actors, doctors and singers, are admired. Do you admire anyone who is famous? Has that admiration influenced your decision about what you want to do with your life?

UNIT FOUR
THE TURTLE
Monolog

Getting Set

Listen to the recording, and write the sentences of the introduction in the lines below.

1. ______________________________ (9 words)
2. ______________________________ (12 words)
3. ______________________________ (6 words)
4. ______________________________ (8 words)

Tuning In

Check to see if you know the meanings of these words from the monolog.

1. *to have a thing for:* (slang) to like a lot
2. *turtle:* a land and sea animal with a hard shell
3. *pet:* an animal which is kept as a friend in the house
4. *to wrap:* to cover with paper

Summing Up

Read these five statements about the monolog. Listen to the recording as many times as you like. Then choose the best answer for each of the statements, and write the letter in the space.

1. Chuck went to a pet shop to buy a ______.
   a. cat
   b. turtle
   c. dog
   d. goldfish
2. Chuck asked the clerk in the pet shop about the pet's ______.
   a. health
   b. food
   c. cage
   d. habits
3. The clerk told Chuck the pet would live ______.
   a. if it were fed
   b. if it were loved
   c. for a short time
   d. for a long time
4. Chuck bought the pet and the next morning ______.
   a. his mother found it
   b. the clerk found it
   c. it was gone
   d. it was dead
5. The clerk told Chuck that the turtle had had a ______.
   a. disease
   b. heart attack
   c. birthday
   d. baby

Retelling

Tell the story in your own words. You may use the sentences below as a guide.

When Chuck was a boy, he liked ______________________________. Once he went to ______________________________. He asked ______________________________ ______________________________. The shopkeeper said ______________________________ ______________________________. So Chuck ______________________________ ______________________________. The next morning ______________________________ ______________________________, so ______________________________. Chuck told ______________________________. The shopkeeper said ______________________________.

Filling In

Listen to the recording, and fill in the blanks. You may listen to the monolog as many times as you need to.

When I was a little kid, I had a real thing for turtles. And one day I ________ (1) into a pet shop, uh, ________ (2) look for a turtle ________ (3) they had a lot ________ (4) different turtles in the ________ (5) shop.

And . . . there was ________ (6) kind of turtle that ________ (7) liked a lot. So ________ (8) asked the shopkeeper, uh, inside ________ (9) shop, uh, if those turtles ________ (10) healthy. And he said, "Oh, ________ (11)," that they were really ________ (12). And I said, "Well, uh, ________ (13) long do you think ________ (14) turtle will live?"

And ________ (15) said, "Oh, it'll probably ________ (16) at least ten thousand ________ (17) and maybe even more."

Uh, ________ (18) that made me really ________ (19). So I told him ________ (20), I'd take it. So ________ (21) put it in a ________ (22) and wrapped it and ________ (23) some holes in it ________ (24) the turtle could get ________ (25) air and I took ________ (26) home.

And the next _________ 27 when I woke up, _________ 28 wanted to go and _________ 29 with my turtle. And _________ 30 went in and looked _________ 31 the turtle bowl, and _________ 32 thing was dead already _________ 33 really made me angry.

_________ 34 I ran back to _________ 35 pet shop and I _________ 36 to the same clerk _________ 37 was there, ''That turtle _________ 38 sold me yesterday's already _________ 39.''

Uh, and the shopkeeper said, ''_________ 40? Oh, that's too bad. _________ 41 guess yesterday was its _________ 42 and it just became _________ 43 thousand years old then.''

ANGER

Discussion

Pairing Up

Work with another student. One of you will be **A,** and the other will be **B.** When you finish the activity, change parts and repeat it. Student **B** may answer with one of the choices, or s/he may provide his/her own response.

Being Angry

STUDENT A: (Ask B if s/he gets angry often.)

____?

STUDENT B: 1. Yes. Especially when I'm *tired/busy/sick.*
2. Now and then I do.

3. ____.

STUDENT A: (Ask B what s/he does when s/he's angry.)

____?

STUDENT B: 1. I don't talk.
2. I don't do anything special.

3. ____.

STUDENT A: (Ask if that's a good way of coping with it.)

____?

STUDENT B: 1. At least it makes me feel better.
2. No. But I don't know what else to do.

3. ____.

Pets

STUDENT A: (Ask B how s/he feels about keeping pets.)

____?

STUDENT B: 1. I like pets a lot.
2. I don't like taking care of them.

3. ____.

STUDENT A: (Ask if s/he ever had a pet of his/her own.)

____?

STUDENT B: 1. Sure. When I was a kid, I had a dog.
2. No. I've never lived in a place where I could.

3. ____.

STUDENT A: (Ask which animals s/he thinks make the best pets.)

____?

STUDENT B: 1. As far as I'm concerned, dogs are the best.
2. I've always liked cats.
3. ______________________________.

Tuning In

Check to see if you know the meanings of these words from the discussion.

1. *mug:* a large cup
2. *tatami:* a Japanese floor mat
3. *gloomy:* very sad
4. *would rather:* prefer to
5. *to duck:* to lower your body or head
6. *to pick up* : to learn without planning to
7. *handy:* convenient
8. *to take* (*it out on*): to express one's feelings by making someone (or something) else suffer
9. *to cope:* to deal successfully
10. *row:* a noisy fight

Summing Up

Read these statements about the discussion. Listen to the recording as many times as you like. Then choose the best answer for each of the statements, and write the letter in the space.

1. When Bette gets angry, she _______.
   a. throws shoes through doors
   b. throws dishes on the floor
   c. drinks a lot of coffee
   d. doesn't talk to her family
2. _______ is surprised that Bette throws things.
   a. Chuck
   b. Gary
   c. Sharon
   d. Everyone
3. When Gary and Sharon get angry, they usually _______.
   a. throw shoes
   b. throw dishes
   c. don't talk
   d. talk a lot
4. Both Sharon's sister and Bette's mother _______ when they get angry.
   a. throw dishes
   b. throw shoes
   c. argue a lot
   d. don't talk
5. Bette shows her anger the way she describes instead of _______.
   a. having an argument with someone
   b. having a discussion with someone
   c. coping with the problem
   d. forgetting about the problem

Retelling

Retell the discussion in your own words. You may use the sentences below as a guide.

The people are talking about what they do when they feel ________________.
The first woman (Bette) ____.
____. The first man (Gary) and the second
woman (Sharon) both ____.
The other man (Chuck) ____
____. Sharon's little sister and Bette's
mother ____.
Bette believes that it's better to ____
rather than ____.

Read the statements below. Listen to the discussion, and think about what the speakers are saying. Then decide if each statement is *possible* or *not probable* because of the information in the discussion. Find some evidence to support your answer.

1. Gary would probably go to a movie when he's angry.
2. Sharon would probably go directly to her teacher instead of complaining to friends if she got a bad grade in a course.
3. When she's angry, Sharon's sister might take a taxi instead of driving.
4. Bette might feel that her way of showing anger is the normal thing to do.
5. Chuck would probably go to a party when he's angry.

Filling In

Listen to the recording, and fill in the blanks. You may listen to the discussion as many times as you need to.

GARY: What do you all do when you're angry? Is there any special ________ (1) that you do?

BETTE: I ________ (2) and throw dishes on ________ (3) floor. And you know ________ (4) really awful is when ________ (5) dishes don't break! (*laughter*)

GARY: You actually . . . you actually throw dishes on the floor?

SHARON: You really throw dishes on the floor?

BETTE: Yes, I ________(6) out these coffee ________(7) I've got and I ________(8) throw it as hard ________(9) I can.

SHARON: What are you going to do on your tatami floor?

BETTE: I don't know.

CHUCK: Wow, I don't want to be around you . . . yeah, I don't want to be around you when you get angry next time.

GARY: Really, I've ________(10) known anybody to do ________(11) . . . you see it in the mo— . . .

SHARON: What do you do, Gary?

GARY: Well, I usually don't ________(12).

SHARON: Really?

GARY: Yeah, I become ________(13) gloomy.

SHARON: I kind of ________(14) the same thing. I ________(15) get quiet.

CHUCK: I just ________(16) to be alone. I'd ________(17) not be around anyone.

SHARON: ________(18) little sister used to ________(19) shoes at people. (*laughter*) . . . Really! ________(20) can't tell you how ________(21) shoes I've had to ________(22).

BETTE: My mother would do ________(23) too, you know. One ________(24) she threw a shoe, uh, ________(25) my brother and it ________(26) right through the door. ________(27) she had to hide ________(28) hole in the door ________(29) my father. (*laughter*)

GARY: How long, ________(30), have you been throwing ________(31) on the floor and ________(32) did you pick this ________(33)?

BETTE: Oh, well . . .

SHARON: From her mother.

BETTE: No, no . . . you know, ________(34) you're in a situation ________(35) you get mad at

________ (36) and they're not available ________ (37) you can't tell them ________ (38) mad you are.

GARY: Mmm . . . mmm . . . mmm . . .

BETTE: Um . . . so ________ (39) next handiest thing is ________ (40) take it out on ________ (41) dishes and actually that's ________ (42) better way of coping ________ (43) it, you know, rather ________ (44) getting into a row ________ (45) someone.

SHARON: Maybe, but it ________ (46) really solve the problem ________ (47) there's a problem.

BETTE: Well, ________ (48), you know, you can ________ (49) a situation, but, uh, (*sigh*) . . . still ________ (50) upset by it.

SHARON: I ________ (51) so.

Speaking Out

Read the discussion suggestions below, and choose one to talk or write about.

1. ANGER: Have you ever been really angry with someone you liked very much? Why were you angry? Did you show your anger? How do you usually solve the problem when you're angry with someone?
2. NOT TALKING: Have you ever refused to talk to a person that you see every day? What was the situation? What happened?
3. PETS: How do you feel about pets? Have you ever had a pet? What was it?
4. ANGER ABOUT SITUATIONS: What kinds of social or public situations, such as riding crowded buses or buying things that are no good, make you angry? Do other people seem to feel the same way?

UNIT FIVE
PAM'S PROBLEM
Monolog

Getting Set

Listen to the recording, and write the sentences of the introduction in the lines below.

1. ______________________________ (7 words)

2. ______________________________ (6 words)

3. ______________________________ (9 words)

4. ______________________________ (8 words)

Tuning In

Check to see if you know the meanings of these words from the monolog.

1. *figure:* the shape of a human body
2. *contest:* a competition
3. *to yell:* to shout

Summing Up

Read these five statements about the monolog. Listen to the recording as many times as you like. Then choose the best answer for each of the statements, and write the letter in the space.

1. Sharon's sister Pam used to have a very ______.
   a. nice house
   b. nice backyard
   c. beautiful sister
   d. beautiful body
2. Now that Pam is married, she is ______ about her appearance.
   a. very careful
   b. not so careful
   c. very happy
   d. not so happy
3. Students used to bother Pam ______.
   a. when she was first married
   b. before she got married
   c. when she was a university student
   d. before she was a university student
4. The students used to ______ Pam.
   a. bring presents for
   b. write letters to
   c. whistle and shout at
   d. talk and visit with
5. The students probably don't bother Pam now because she doesn't ______.
   a. like the students
   b. know the students
   c. look like she did before
   d. look like someone they know

Retelling

Tell the story in your own words. You may use the sentences below as a guide.

Sharon's sister Pam used to ______________________________,

but now she ______________________________. When Pam

first got married, the university students ______________________________

______________________________. She doesn't understand ______

______________________________.

Filling In

Listen to the recording, and fill in the blanks. You may listen to the monolog as many times as you need to.

My sister Pam had a really beautiful figure when she was younger because, uh, she used to pay a lot of attention to the things she ate and she didn't eat a whole lot. And a couple of ______ (1) she would enter, uh, local ______ (2) contests and stuff, swimming ______ (3) stuff and she had ______ (4) kind of a nice ______ (5). But she got married ______ (6) she had a couple ______ (7) kids and she's not ______ (8) as thin as she ______ (9) to be. As a ______ (10) of fact, uh, sometimes she ______ (11) pay very much attention ______ (12) the way she looks ______ (13) all.

And we were talking ______ (14) other day and she ______ (15) telling me that when ______ (16) first got married, the ______ (17) at the university next ______ (18) her house used to ______ (19) give her a hard ______ (20) when she went out to . . . to ______ (21) in the summertime. And ______ (22) would whistle and yell ______ (23) sometimes she really had ______ (24) just go in the ______ (25). And she said, "You ______ (26), that really doesn't happen ______ (27) often anymore. I ______ (28) don't understand why."

And ______ (29) looked at her and ______ (30) said, "Really?"

NUDITY IN ART

Discussion

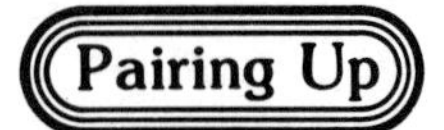

Work with another student. One of you will be **A,** and the other will be **B.** When you finish the activity, change parts and repeat it. Student **B** may answer with one of the choices, or s/he may provide his/her own response.

Nudity in Art

STUDENT A: (Ask B how s/he feels about nudity in art.)

____?

STUDENT B: 1. I'm for it.
2. I'm against it.

3. ____.

STUDENT A: (Ask if s/he feels strange looking at nude art.)

____?

STUDENT B: 1. Maybe a little.
2. No, not at all.

3. ____.

STUDENT A: (Ask if s/he would paint nudes if s/he were an artist.)

____?

STUDENT B: 1. Yeah. I think I'd try.
2. No, probably not.

3. ____.

Censorship

STUDENT A: (Ask B what his/her feelings on censorship are.)

____?

STUDENT B: 1. I don't like censorship of any kind.
2. I think some censorship is necessary.

3. ____.

STUDENT A: (Ask if there's censorship in his/her country.)

____?

STUDENT B: 1. Yes, to a certain extent.
2. No, none at all.

3. ____.

STUDENT A: (Ask who s/he thinks should decide what should be censored.)

____?

STUDENT B: 1. The government.
2. The people.
3. ______________________________.

Tuning In

Check to see if you know the meanings of these words from the discussion.

1. *nude:* without clothes
2. *to be for:* to feel positive about
3. *parochial:* narrow
4. *ultimate:* greatest
5. *challenge:* work which requires dedication
6. *to portray:* to make a representation of someone (or something) in painting, drawing, etc.
7. *to recline:* to lie down
8. *to object to:* to disagree with
9. *touching* : causing emotion

Summing Up

Read these statements about the discussion. Listen to the recording as many times as you like. Then choose the best answer for each of the statements, and write the letter in the space.

1. Bette is interested in experimenting with nude ______.
   a. photography
   b. painting
   c. sculpture
   d. drawing
2. Chuck doesn't understand how anyone could object to ______.
   a. Greek statues
   b. nude photography
   c. seeing Goya's nude
   d. seeing Goya nude
3. Bette and Chuck feel there's no difference between ______.
   a. Michelangelo and Goya
   b. painting and photography
   c. modern art and other kinds of art
   d. nude art and other kinds of art
4. Sharon tells about an artist who ______ because he did nude paintings.
   a. lost his job
   b. lost his friends
   c. became famous
   d. had many problems
5. Bette says that people should understand that painting pictures of the nude body is ______ an artist.
   a. an impossibility for
   b. a challenge to
   c. an honor for
   d. a disgrace to

Retell the discussion in your own words. You may use the sentences below as a guide.

The people are talking about ____.

The first woman (Bette) would like to ____.

The second woman (Sharon) remembers that when she was in college, ______________

____.

A few years ago, the first man (Chuck) ____

____.

The second man (Gary) asked if ____

____. Bette said that she feels the

same about ____.

Drawing Out

Read the statements below. Listen to the discussion, and think about what the speakers are saying. Then decide if each statement is *possible* or *not probable* because of the information in the discussion. Find some evidence to support your answer.

1. Bette might have thought about this topic frequently.
2. Sharon probably thinks school principals should not tell teachers what to do.
3. Chuck might think certain books and magazines should not be sold.
4. Bette might cry at sad movies.
5. Sharon might choose movies carefully.

Filling In

Listen to the recording, and fill in the blanks. You may listen to the discussion as many times as you need to.

CHUCK: How do you feel about nudity in art? Does it bother you?

GARY: I'm for it.

CHUCK: Or do you have any special feeling ________ (1) anything?

BETTE: Oh, I really ________ (2) it. As a matter ________ (3) fact, I'd like to ________ (4) with taking artistic photographs . . . of, of ________ (5), nude males.

CHUCK: Really?

GARY: Really?

SHARON: I never thought about ________ (6) a lot, you kn— . . . in ________ (7) college it was quite ________ (8) problem at one time. It . . .

CHUCK: Why would your college . . .

BETTE: You mean you had a lot of students running around nude? (*laughter*)

SHARON: No, but one of ________ (9) artists on the, in ________ (10) art department had done ________ (11), some paintings and he ________ (12) his wife as a ________ (13). It disturbed a lot ________ (14) people.

BETTE: Oh, well, you know ________ (15), that's, that, that's really very parochial ________ (16), because the n—, nude body ________ (17) supposed to be the ________ (18) challenge to an artist . . .

SHARON: Well, I, I . . .

BETTE: . . . to be able ________ (19) portray . . .

SHARON: Yeah.

BETTE: . . . meaningfully.

SHARON: I think so too, but I, I guess ________ (20) depends on how it's ________ (21) too.

CHUCK: Well, a few ________ (22) ago I saw a ________ (23) famous nude, uh, Goya's nude . . . a reclining lady.

SHARON: Did you, oh, did you see that here?

CHUCK: Yeah, one of the ________ (24) beautiful paintings I've ever ________ (25).

SHARON: Hah!

CHUCK: Uh, I don't see how ________ (26) person could object to ________ (27) like that.

GARY: Do you ________ (28) feel strange, any of ________ (29), you know, looking at a, a ________ (30) painting or nude statue? ________ (31), for example, you were ________ (32) a big room someplace ________ (33) there were a, there ________ (34) a Greek . . . or

Michelangelo statue . . .

BETTE: I feel, oh, I . . . I feel strange only ________ (35) that, if it's something ________ (36) so incredibly beautiful and ________ (37) done, it's very touching ________ (38), uh, somebody, to think ________ (39) somebody could actually do that . . .

SHARON: Well, I . . .

CHUCK: But couldn't ________ (40) feel that same way ________ (41) any piece of art ________ (42)?

BETTE: Oh, yeah . . .

CHUCK: Which means that you don't really overreact . . . yeah . . .

BETTE: . . . well, I don't make a distinction between ________ (43) and other kinds.

CHUCK: Yeah, that's good.

Speaking Out

Read the discussion suggestions below, and choose one to talk or write about.

1. NUDITY IN ART: How do you feel about nudity in art? When viewing nude art, do you feel the same as when looking at non-nude art?
2. CHILDREN'S QUESTIONS: Did you ever ask a question and get the answer, "You're too young to understand" from your parents? When you speak to children, do you ever say that? Why or why not?
3. AGING: How do you feel about getting older? What things seem to be more important to older people? What things seem to be more important to younger people? Why?
4. PHYSICAL BEAUTY: Is the way a person looks important to you when you make friends? How important is it after you get to know a person? Why?
5. HONESTY: What does being honest mean to you? Do you think you are usually honest with yourself and with others? Why do you think so?

UNIT SIX
THE TEMPERATURE CHECK
Monolog

Getting Set

Listen to the recording, and write the sentences of the introduction in the lines below.

1. ____ (10 words)
2. ____ (10 words)
3. ____ (9 words)
4. ____ (7 words)

Tuning In

Check to see if you know the meanings of these words from the monolog.

1. *disc jockey:* a person who plays records and talks on a radio program
2. *up:* awake

Summing Up

Read these five statements about the monolog. Listen to the recording as many times as you like. Then choose the best answer for each of the statements, and write the letter in the space.

1. Sharon was ______ one night last winter.
   a. listening to a radio program
   b. watching TV
   c. washing clothes
   d. washing dishes

2. The disc jockey told his listeners to check their temperatures and ______.
   a. call Sharon
   b. call an old lady
   c. call the radio station
   d. call the weather office

3. An old woman called and ______ her temperature.
   a. told the disc jockey
   b. asked the disc jockey
   c. told Sharon
   d. asked Sharon

4. The woman thought the disc jockey was asking about ______.
   a. air temperature
   b. body temperature
   c. the amount of water in the air
   d. the amount of pollution in the air

5. The disc jockey was really asking about ______.
   a. air temperature
   b. body temperature
   c. the amount of water in the air
   d. the amount of pollution in the air

Retelling

Tell the story in your own words. You may use the sentences below as a guide.

One night, Sharon was ____________________.

The disc jockey wanted his audience to ____________________

____________________. Soon, an old lady ____________

____________________. She told everyone ____________________

____________________ instead of ____________________.

Filling In

Listen to the recording, and fill in the blanks. You may listen to the monolog as many times as you need to.

Last winter we had kind of a, uh, cold winter and I was home in bed reading one night and listening to my radio. And, uh, ________ (1) disc jockey who . . . was ________ (2) of an interesting guy ________ (3) would . . . he would play ________ (4) and talk to his ________ (5) audience, uh, announced that it ________ (6), uh, about eight degrees outside ________ (7) radio station.

And then ________ (8) went on to say ________ (9) he was a little ________ (10) about the temperature in ________ (11) rest of the city ________ (12) if people were up, ________ (13) didn't they check their ________ (14) and . . . and call in to ________ (15) station, tell him how ________ (16) it was where they ________ (17), and then he would ________ (18) it to everybody else ________ (19) to his program.

And . . . well, ________ (20) was sort of comfortable ________ (21) I didn't get up, ________ (22) I . . . kept listening to ________ (23) radio station and couple ________ (24) minutes later somebody called ________ (25) and it was a ________ (26) of funny little old ________ (27). We could hear her ________ (28), of course, over the ________ (29).

And she said, "Well, ________ (30) checked my temperature and ________ (31) normal just like always . . . ________ (32)-eight point six."

INFORMATION
Discussion

Pairing Up

Work with another student. One of you will be **A,** and the other will be **B.** When you finish the activity, change parts and repeat it. Student **B** may answer with one of the choices, or s/he may provide his/her own response.

Keeping Up

STUDENT A: (Ask B if s/he tries to keep up with world events.)

____?

STUDENT B: 1. Yeah. I try to keep up, but it's hard.
2. No. I don't even try to keep up.
3. ____.

STUDENT A: (Ask how s/he knows what's going on.)

____?

STUDENT B: 1. By reading a lot.
2. By listening to the radio.
3. ____.

STUDENT A: (Ask if s/he feels s/he has to keep up.)

____?

STUDENT B: 1. Yeah. I think I ought to try.
2. No. I don't even try.
3. ____.

Being Responsible

STUDENT A: (Ask B if s/he is a responsible person.)

____?

STUDENT B: 1. Yeah. At least I try to be.
2. No. I don't even try to be.
3. ____.

STUDENT A: (Ask if s/he wants to contribute to society.)

____?

STUDENT B: 1. Yeah. I think everyone should try to.
2. I'm not sure if I have anything to contribute.
3. ____.

STUDENT A: (Ask if s/he has to be informed to do that.)

____?

STUDENT B: 1. Yeah. Generally you have to.
2. No. Generally you don't have to.

3. ____.

Tuning In

Check to see if you know the meanings of these words from the discussion.

1. *dumb* : stupid
2. *field* : a subject for study, usually related to your job
3. *pressed* : forced
4. *to keep up with* : to stay informed about
5. *source* : the place where you find information

Summing Up

Read these statements about the discussion. Listen to the recording as many times as you like. Then choose the best answer for each of the statements, and write the letter in the space.

1. Bette says that people today are interested in the whole world because of ______.
   a. good methods of transportation
   b. good systems of communication
   c. the United Nations
   d. the Common Market
2. Sharon says that ______ should know about international events.
   a. teachers
   b. high school students
   c. university students
   d. educated adults
3. ______ says you have to be able to trust the places your information comes from.
   a. Bette
   b. Chuck
   c. Gary
   d. Sharon
4. Bette feels everyone should ______.
   a. contribute to charity
   b. attend international events
   c. travel to other countries
   d. know what's happening in the world
5. Everyone in this discussion feels that keeping up with general knowledge and international events is their ______.
   a. privilege
   b. challenge
   c. responsibility
   d. recreation

Retelling

Retell the discussion in your own words. You may use the sentences below as a guide.

The first woman (Bette) says that she can't ____

________________. The first man (Gary) agrees that this is a problem

because ________________. Bette says that

in the past, ________________

________________, but now ________________.

The other man (Chuck) thinks it's impossible to ________________

________________. The other woman (Sharon) believes

that a responsible person ________________

________________. Gary says that we must be

able to choose ________________, and Chuck adds that we must

be able to ________________.

Drawing Out

Read the statements below. Listen to the discussion, and think about what the speakers are saying. Then decide if each statement is *possible* or *not probable* because of the information in the discussion. Find some evidence to support your answer.

1. Bette might think that she is a slow reader.
2. Gary might try to read more than one newspaper every day.
3. The language used in this discussion is difficult because of the subject.
4. Bette and Sharon probably vote in every election.
5. Chuck and Gary might read every page of the newspaper.

Filling In

Listen to the recording, and fill in the blanks. You may listen to the discussion as many times as you need to.

BETTE: You know, I feel ______ (1) dumb. Um, there's so much ______ (2) I don't know and ______ (3) much happening and so ______ (4) to read that I . . . I ______ (5) process all the information ______ (6). Do y'all feel the same way?

GARY: I . . . I know . . . yeah, I know what you ______ (7) . . . There, there's so much to ______ (8) out about in so ______ (9) different ways nowadays. We ______ (10) television, we have radio, ________(11) have all sorts of ________(12).

SHARON: Even in your own ________(13), you know, you'd have ________(14) read twenty or thirty ________(15) a month in order ________(16) keep up.

CHUCK: Just to ________(17) what's happening, that's right.

SHARON: Yeah.

CHUCK: And ________(18) so when you consider ________(19) whole world.

BETTE: Yeah, that's ________(20) thing. You know, now, ________(21) before, our sphere of ________(22) was maybe just our ________(23) or our area, because ________(24) communications systems, uh, your sphere ________(25) interest is the whole ________(26).

CHUCK: Yeah, yeah, that's right.

GARY: And before, people didn't realize ________(27) they sh—, I . . . I think we ________(28) now that we should ________(29) things. And therefore, we ________(30) pressed to know these ________(31) . . .

BETTE: Well, we're . . .

GARY: . . . whereas people before didn't ________(32) that.

CHUCK: But, I think, uh, ________(33) physically impossible, uh, to keep ________(34) with everything that's going ________(35) all the time. And ________(36) think in our own ________(37) we've got to realize ________(38), that we just can't do ________(39). And then work from ________(40) . . . somehow.

SHARON: But at the ________(41) time you feel that ________(42), you think that as ________(43) . . . educated adult, you have ________(44) keep up with . . . with certain ________(45) events and affairs or ________(46) not really be a ________(47) person.

BETTE: Yeah . . . yeah, you know that, that's it . . . it's your responsibility in ________(48) decisions about not only ________(49) own life, but, you ________(50), uh, other things, contributing in ________ (51) way and you have ________ (52) be informed to be ________ (53) to do that.

GARY: You ________ (54) to learn to pick ________ (55) choose information too.

BETTE: Yeah.

SHARON: Or ________ (56) faster. (*laughter*)

CHUCK: Yeah, that's a ________ (57) point though, picking and ________ (58) information, like . . . and being ________ (59) to depend on the ________ (60) of your information.

SHARON: Really.

Speaking Out

Read the discussion suggestions below, and choose one to talk or write about.

1. INFORMATION: Do you try to keep up with any special area of knowledge? If so, what books, magazines, etc., do you read? Is it difficult to keep up with your reading?
2. LISTENING TO THE RADIO: Do you like to listen to the radio? When do you usually listen? What kind of programs do you like best? Why?
3. SEASONS: What is your favorite season? Why? Which would you like better, living in a place with four seasons or living in a place with only one season? Why?
4. FEELING DUMB: Do you sometimes feel dumb? What makes you feel dumb? Are there times when "playing dumb" is a good thing to do? Why?
5. CONTRIBUTING TO SOCIETY: Bette said that educated adults should contribute to society. Do you agree? Why? How can the average person contribute to society?

UNIT SEVEN
TIMMY'S CHOICE
Monolog

Getting Set

Listen to the recording, and write the sentences of the introduction in the lines below.

1. ______________________________ (7 words)

2. ______________________________ (8 words)

3. ______________________________ (8 words)

4. ______________________________ (8 words)

Tuning In

Check to see if you know the meanings of these words from the monolog.

1. *to put up with:* to tolerate
2. *hand-me-down clothes:* clothes used by one person after the clothes were used by another
3. *to share:* to use something together with someone else
4. *pregnant:* going to have a baby
5. *heart-to-heart:* sincere
6. *pony:* small horse

Summing Up

Read these statements about the monolog. Listen to the recording as many times as you like. Then choose the best answer for each of the statements, and write the letter in the space.

1. Timmy was the ______ child in his family.
   a. youngest
   b. oldest
   c. best-behaved
   d. worst-behaved

2. He'd always had to ______ everything.
   a. clean
   b. share
   c. wash
   d. eat

3. Finally he was given ______.
   a. some new toys
   b. some new clothes
   c. a room of his own
   d. a pony of his own

4. When his mother got pregnant again, Timmy's father ______.
   a. gave Timmy his own room
   b. gave Timmy a pony
   c. talked to Timmy's mother
   d. talked to Timmy

5. Timmy wanted a pony because ______.
   a. his older sister had one
   b. his friends had one
   c. he didn't want his own room
   d. he didn't want to share his room

Retelling

Tell the story in your own words. You may use the sentences below as a guide.

In Timmy's family, there are ____.
Since he is the youngest, ____
____________________. When Timmy finally got his own room, ____________
____. Timmy's father asked him
______________________________, and Timmy said ________________________
____.

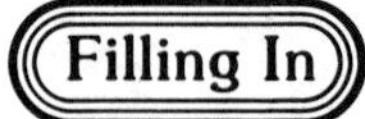

Listen to the recording, and fill in the blanks. You may listen to the monolog as many times as you need to.

Little Timmy's only seven years old and he comes from a big family. He's got six brothers and sisters. Being the youngest, ________ (1) always had to put ________ (2) with taking hand-me-________ (3) clothes and waiting until ________ (4) bowls at the dinner ________ (5) get to him last ________ (6) really having to share ________ (7). Uh, finally, after sharing most ________ (8) including clothes and even ________ (9) room, he got his ________ (10) room. But it didn't ________ (11) very long because his ________ (12) became pregnant again. So ________ (13) father thought that he ________ (14) sit down with Timmy ________ (15) have a heart-to-________ (16) talk and his father ________ (17) him, "Timmy, which would ________ (18) prefer, another brother or ________ (19) sister?"

And Timmy ________ (20), "Well, if it's all ________ (21) with you and Mom, ________ (22) about just a pony?"

STINGINESS
Discussion

Pairing Up

Work with another student. One of you will be **A,** and the other will be **B.** When you finish the activity, change parts and repeat it. Student **B** may answer with one of the choices, or s/he may provide his/her own response.

Being Stingy

STUDENT A: (Ask B if s/he has friends who are stingy.)

____?

STUDENT B: 1. Yes. I have *many/a few* like that.
2. No. I don't have any like that.

3. ____.

STUDENT A: (Ask if s/he knows what makes people stingy.)

____?

STUDENT B: 1. Maybe they're born that way.
2. Maybe they learned it as little kids.

3. ____.

STUDENT A: (Ask if s/he thinks s/he's a stingy person.)

____?

STUDENT B: 1. Yes, actually, I guess I am.
2. No, I don't think so.

3. ____.

Family

STUDENT A: (Ask B if s/he has any brothers and sisters.)

____?

STUDENT B: 1. Yes. I have _______________________________________.
2. No. I'm an only child.

3. ____.

STUDENT A: (Ask how that was when s/he was growing up.)

____?

STUDENT B: 1. It was good. I had somebody to play with.
2. It wasn't so good. I didn't have anyone to play with.

3. ____.

STUDENT A: (Ask about now.)

____?

STUDENT B: 1. It's great. We all try to help each other out.
2. I regret not coming from a bigger family.
3. ______________________________.

Tuning In

Check to see if you know the meanings of these words from the discussion.

1. *stingy:* not liking to spend money
2. *thrifty:* careful about money

Summing Up

Read these statements about the discussion. Listen to the recording as many times as you like. Then choose the best answer for each of the statements, and write the letter in the space.

1. ______ said there is often a confusion of two ideas: stinginess and thriftiness.
   a. Bette
   b. Chuck
   c. Gary
   d. Sharon
2. Everyone agreed that people who ______ are stingy.
   a. buy for others and never for themselves
   b. buy for themselves and not for others
   c. save money for a special purpose
   d. spend money for no reason
3. Bette thought her boyfriend was stingy because he ______.
   a. tried to save money
   b. wanted to impress her
   c. bought roses
   d. bought paper flowers
4. Sharon's sister was ______ as a child but has become ______ as an adult.
   a. stingy . . . generous
   b. generous . . . stingy
   c. poor . . . thrifty
   d. thrifty . . . poor
5. Chuck pointed out that some people are a combination of ______.
   a. funny and serious
   b. poor and honest
   c. thrifty and stingy
   d. stingy and poor

Retelling

Retell the discussion in your own words. You may use the sentences below as a guide.

The first woman (Bette) had a boyfriend who was ______________________.

He bought her ______________________ because ______________________

______________________. Bette would have preferred ______________________.

The other woman (Sharon) asked if Bette thought ______________________________

______________________, and Bette said ______________________________.

Sharon said that one of her sisters used to be ______________________________,

but now ____.

Bette wanted to know ______________________________________.

One man (Gary) said that people sometimes confuse the words ______________

and ______________________. Bette added that a person might not spend money

because ____

____.

Drawing Out

Read the statements below. Listen to the discussion again, and think about what the speakers are saying. Then decide if each statement is *possible* or *not probable* because of the information in the discussion. Find some evidence to support your answer.

1. Sharon has probably lived away from home for a long time.
2. Bette might feel that a person who gives inexpensive gifts is a stingy person.
3. Gary might have more than one bank account.
4. Chuck has probably never thought much about the difference between being stingy and being thrifty.
5. Bette might have been very angry when she received the paper flowers.

Filling In

Listen to the recording, and fill in the blanks. You may listen to the discussion as many times as you need to.

BETTE: You know, I used to have this boyfriend who was so stingy that he bought me paper flowers 'cause they would last longer. (*laughter*)

SHARON: Really?

CHUCK: Well, that's a good idea.

GARY: That's pretty stingy. That's pretty stingy. When you receive a ________ (1) like that, apparently you ________ (2) affected by it, you would ________ (3) felt better, wouldn't you, ________ (4) you received, uh, real flowers?

BETTE: Well, roses, of course.

SHARON: Did you think it was funny at the time?

BETTE: Well, ________(5) did because this person ________(6) so stingy that even ________(7) him to buy paper ________(8) (*laughter*) was being generous for ________(9). (*laughter*)

SHARON: Oh, Lord. You know, my . . . some ________(10) and brothers have grown ________(11) since I've known them ________(12) I was very interested ________(13) hear my mother talking ________(14) how stingy one of ________(15) sisters is who used ________(16) be very generous. I ________(17) it's very interesting.

CHUCK: Mmm . . . mmm . . .

BETTE: I wonder what makes people stingy.

GARY: Well, ________(18) it's a confusion of ________(19). A person, I think, ________(20) be stingy. Then a ________(21) can be thrifty. And ________(22) many times those two ________(23) are, uh . . .

BETTE: Yeah.

GARY: . . . confused.

BETTE: And a person can be poor too.

GARY: And poor.

CHUCK: Yeah, yeah, but sometimes the . . . the ________(24) a combination of those ________(25), I feel.

SHARON: Stingy and ________(26), or stingy and thrifty?

CHUCK: Stingy and thrifty.

GARY: Give an example.

CHUCK: Give an example?

GARY: Mmm-hmm. You mean, uh, like ________(27) person has money and, uh, ________(28) wants to buy something ________(29) maybe he doesn't buy ________(30) because he's saving his ______ (31) for . . .

BETTE: Or he buys ______ (32) himself, but he doesn't ______ (33) for others.

GARY: Oh, now that's ______ (34).

BETTE: Yeah, well . . .

CHUCK: Yeah, that's definitely stingy.

GARY: That's not thrifty. That's stingy.

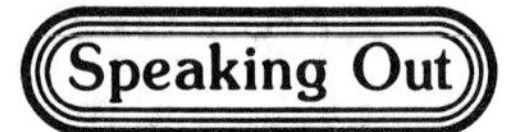

Read the discussion suggestions below, and choose one to talk or write about.

1. BEING STINGY: What do you think makes a person generous or stingy? Do you have friends who are very generous or very stingy? Why do you think they are this way?
2. DECIDING WHO PAYS: When you go out with friends, how do you decide who should take care of the money? When do you pay for another person? When do other people pay for you? Do you think the man should always pay for the woman?
3. FRIENDS: What kinds of things would you do for a friend or expect a friend to do for you? Do you often ask friends to do things for you? Do you always try to do things for yourself? Why?
4. BROTHERS AND SISTERS: Do you have any brothers or sisters? How do you get along with them? What kinds of things do you share with them?
5. CONFUSION OF WORDS: Do you sometimes confuse words in English? Which words?

UNIT EIGHT
JUDGE BROWN'S CAR
Monolog

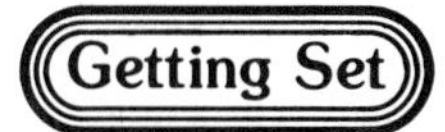

Listen to the recording, and write the sentences of the introduction in the lines below.

1. ______________________________ (12 words)
2. ______________________________ (7 words)
3. ______________________________ (7 words)
4. ______________________________ (9 words)

Tuning In

Check to see if you know the meanings of these words from the monolog.

1. *no-parking zone:* a place where parking is illegal
2. *to tow:* to pull with a truck

Read these five statements about the monolog. Listen to the recording as many times as you like. Then choose the best answer for each of the statements, and write the letter in the space.

1. The policeman told Judge Brown about a car ______.
   a. in a no-parking zone
   b. in a parking lot
   c. that was stolen
   d. that was damaged
2. The policeman said the owner of the car was an ______ person.
   a. industrious
   b. honest
   c. earnest
   d. important
3. Judge Brown said the car should be ______.
   a. given away
   b. taken away
   c. destroyed
   d. examined
4. Judge Brown later learned the policeman had been talking about ______ car.
   a. Judge Brown's friend's
   b. Judge Brown's wife's
   c. Judge Brown's
   d. Judge Brown's secretary's
5. Judge Brown thought he didn't have to ______.
   a. obey the law
   b. talk to the policeman
   c. tell the clerk he was going to lunch
   d. tell the policeman he was sorry

Retelling

Tell the story in your own words. You may use the sentences below as a guide.

A policeman asked Judge Brown ______________________________

______________________________. The judge said ______________________________

______________________________.

Later, the judge couldn't ______________________________.

The policeman told him ______________________________.

Filling In

Listen to the recording, and fill in the blanks. You may listen to the monolog as many times as you need to.

I was working as a legal clerk in Judge Brown's office for a long time and a rather funny thing happened one day. Uh, one of the policemen who ______ (1) in, uh, the town came in ______ (2) the judge and said, "______ (3), you know, there's a ______ (4) parked in a no-______ (5) zone and it belongs ______ (6) a rather important person. ______ (7) do you think I ______ (8) do?"

And the judge ______ (9), "Well, the law's the ______ (10). If it's in a ______ (11)-parking zone, surely you ______ (12) to tow it away."

______ (13) the policeman left and ______ (14) guess he towed it ______ (15). Little while later Judge ______ (16) went out for lunch ______ (17) he came back and ______ (18) said, "Where's my car?"

______ (19) I said, "Well, I ______ (20) know," and, uh, just then ______ (21) policeman came back and, uh, ______ (22) policeman said, "Are you ______ (23) for your car?"

And ______ (24) Brown said, "Yeah, wh—, where ______ (25) it?"

And he said, ______ (26) policeman said, "Well, it ______ (27) your car that was ______ (28) the no-parking zone. ______ (29) very sorry."

PRESCRIPTION DRUGS
Discussion

Pairing Up

Work with another student. One of you will be **A,** and the other will be **B.** When you finish the activity, change parts and repeat it. Student **B** may answer with one of the choices, or s/he may provide his/her own response.

Medicine

STUDENT A: (Ask B if we depend on medicine too much.)

____?

STUDENT B: 1. Yes, I think we do.
2. No, I don't think we do.
3. ____.

STUDENT A: (Ask if we could get by without some of it.)

____?

STUDENT B: 1. Yes, I think we could.
2. No, I don't think we could.
3. ____.

STUDENT A: (Ask how often s/he uses medicine.)

____?

STUDENT B: 1. I often use it.
2. I hardly ever use it.
3. ____.

Drug Control

STUDENT A: (Ask B if the drug laws are strict in his/her country.)

____?

STUDENT B: 1. Yes, they're very strict.
2. No, they're not strict at all.
3. ____.

STUDENT A: (Ask if s/he thinks that's good.)

____?

STUDENT B: 1. Yes, I do.
2. No, I don't.
3. ____.

STUDENT A: (Ask who s/he thinks should decide about drugs.)

____?

STUDENT B: 1. It should be up to the government.
2. It should be up to the individual.
3. ______________________________.

Tuning In

Check to see if you know the meanings of these words from the discussion.

1. *prescription:* a doctor's written instructions for the preparation of medicine
2. *to get by :* to manage alone
3. *hypochondriac:* a person who always thinks s/he is sick
4. *antibiotic:* a drug like penicillin
5. *overdose:* too much medicine at one time

Summing Up

Read these statements about the discussion. Listen to the recording as many times as you like. Then choose the best answer for each of the statements, and write the letter in the space.

1. Gary tried to buy some cold medicine, but he couldn't because ______.
   a. he forgot the name
   b. he needed a prescription
   c. he didn't have enough money
   d. the store didn't have it
2. Chuck and Gary think there are certain kinds of drugs that ______.
   a. should be controlled
   b. should be easily bought
   c. everyone should use
   d. no one should use
3. Bette thinks that ______ should be able to choose what drugs to use.
   a. the druggist
   b. the salesclerk
   c. the doctor
   d. the individual
4. Sharon told Chuck about someone ______ vitamin C.
   a. who didn't buy enough
   b. who didn't use enough
   c. who bought too much
   d. who used too much
5. Gary says that if too many antibiotics are used, ______.
   a. they give extra help to the body
   b. they don't help the body
   c. they become very expensive
   d. the drugstore makes a lot of money

Retelling

Retell the discussion in your own words. You may use the sentences below as a guide.

The first man (Gary) went to a drugstore to ______________________________

______________________________. But the druggist ______________

____ because ____________

____.

The second man (Chuck) thinks ________________________________

________________________________. On the other hand, the second woman (Bette) believes ____.

The first woman (Sharon) asks Bette if ____________________________

____________________________, and Bette says ____________________

____.

In Chuck's opinion, ____

________________________________. Gary adds that prescriptions are necessary for ____________________________because ____________________

____________________________. Chuck remembers that Sharon told him about someone who ____. But finally, Sharon agrees with Bette that ________________________________.

Drawing Out

Read the statements below. Listen to the discussion again, and think about what the speakers are saying. Then decide if each statement is *possible* or *not probable* because of the information in the discussion. Find some evidence to support your answer.

1. Bette would probably allow her teenage son to start smoking if he wanted to.
2. Chuck probably takes aspirin every time he has a headache.
3. Gary probably thinks most people should choose their own medicine.
4. Bette might read the small print very carefully on the labels of cans of food.
5. Gary probably thinks he knows a lot about medicine.

Filling In

Listen to the recording, and fill in the blanks. You may listen to the discussion as many times as you need to.

GARY: You know, the other day I went to a drugstore trying to find medicine that I needed for a cold and the . . . the druggist wouldn't sell it to me.

SHARON: Really?

GARY: Yeah.

SHARON: Didn't he ________ (1) it?

GARY: Yeah, he had ________ (2). And it was the ________ (3) of medicine I had ________ (4) before but, uh, apparently now ________ (5) have to have a ________ (6) from the doctor to ________ (7) it.

CHUCK: But I think ________ (8) good . . . because I think ________ (9) people depend on . . . medicines ________ (10) much when they could ________ (11) by without taking stuff.

GARY: Mmm . . .

BETTE: Well, I ________ (12), but, uh, (*sigh*) you know, I ________ (13) really think you should ________ (14) laws against any kind ________ (15) a drug. I think ________ (16) choice should be up ________ (17) the individual. And if ________ (18) person is really a ________ (19), it doesn't make any ________ (20) whether you have to ________ (21) a doctor's prescription or ________ (22).

SHARON: Really?

BETTE: Sure.

SHARON: But if you don't ________ (23) what it is and ________ (24) can go in and ________ (25) anything, don't you think ________ (26) would be some trouble?

BETTE: ________ (27) don't think so. I ________ (28), people don't know what ________ (29) take now, even with ________ (30) doctor's prescription.

CHUCK: Well, I ________ (31) with you that . . . the ________ (32) certainly should be freer ________ (33) drugs, but I do ________ (34) that there're some drugs . . . ________ (35) medicinal things . . . I'm thinking ________ (36) now, like, for example, ________ (37) medicine that Gary was ________ (38) about that I do ________ (39) ought to be sort ________ (40) controlled.

GARY: Sure, uh, the antibiotic ________ (41), in general, if you ________ (42) a lot of them,

__________ (43) a while your system __________ (44) immune to all helps __________ (45) the drugs can give __________ (46). That's why there's a __________ (47) needed.

SHARON: But I thi—. . .

CHUCK: Sharon, you told __________ (48) recently about somebody who __________ (49) an overdose of vitamin __________ (50). People are taking a __________ (51) of vitamin C and __________ (52) took too much. That __________ (53) happen to anybody. Didn't you tell me that?

SHARON: Yeah, it could happen to __________ (54), of course.

BETTE: But you know what . . .

SHARON: I think maybe I agree with Bette __________ (55), I mean, why should __________ (56) be a law against __________ (57)?

CHUCK: You mean drugs of __________ (58) kind.

Speaking Out

Read the discussion suggestions below, and choose one to talk or write about.

1. LAWS ABOUT MEDICINE: How do you feel about having to have a prescription to buy medicine? Should there be laws about selling medicine? Why or why not?
2. AIR POLLUTION: Do you think the problem of cars and air pollution can ever be solved? If you were in a position to do something about this problem, what would you do? What can you do now?
3. BEING CONSERVATIVE OR LIBERAL: Are you generally conservative or are you liberal? Can you give examples? How about most people in your country?
4. IMPORTANT PEOPLE AND THE LAW: Do you think laws are sometimes different for important people? Are you in favor of that? Why or why not?
5. DEATH AND DYING: Have you ever thought about death? How do you feel about that? Are you afraid of it?

UNIT NINE
STEVE'S ROOM
Monolog

Getting Set

Listen to the recording, and write the sentences of the introduction in the lines below.

1. ____ (8 words)

2. ____ (8 words)

3. ____ (11 words)

4. ____ (8 words)

Tuning In

Check to see if you know the meanings of these words from the monolog.

1. *to give in:* to stop refusing
2. *catchall:* a place to keep different kinds of things
3. *storage room:* a room to keep things that you aren't using
4. *to fix up:* to put in order
5. *rash:* without thinking about the results
6. *storm:* weather with strong winds and rain or snow
7. *thunder:* the loud sound during a storm
8. *lightning:* the natural electric light during a storm

Summing Up

Read these five statements about the monolog. Listen to the recording as many times as you like. Then choose the best answer for each of the statements, and write the letter in the space.

1. Steve ______ when he was six years old.
   a. got his own room
   b. got a baby sister
   c. had a lot of friends
   d. had a lot of toys

2. There was a bad thunderstorm ______ Steve slept in his new room.
   a. a few days after
   b. a few weeks after
   c. the second night
   d. the first night

3. He had ______ experienced a thunderstorm before this one.
   a. never
   b. once
   c. often
   d. hardly ever

4. Steve thought that his new room was always ______.
   a. clean
   b. dirty
   c. noisy
   d. quiet

5. He thought that his parents gave him the room because ______.
   a. everybody else wanted it
   b. nobody else wanted it
   c. he promised to keep it clean
   d. he promised to take care of it

Retelling

Tell the story in your own words. You may use the sentences below as a guide.

When Steve was six years old, he decided that ______________________________

______________________________. His father finally agreed,

so they ______________________________.

The first night that Steve slept in his new room, ______________________________

______________________________. His parents went to

his room because ______________________________.

But Steve just felt ______________________________. He thought that they gave

him that room because ______________________________.

Filling In

Listen to the recording, and fill in the blanks. You may listen to the monolog as many times as you need to.

My cousin Steve was six years old when he got his own room. Since the birth of

______ (1) younger sister, he'd been ______ (2) a room with her. ______ (3) school he

heard from ______ (4) of his friends that ______ (5) all had their own ______ (6).

Naturally, after hearing this ______ (7) decided that he, too, ______ (8) his own room.

Uh, he ______ (9) telling his mother and ______ (10) as often as possible

______ (11) he wanted a final—, wanted ______ (12) private room.

Finally his ______ (13) gave in. There was ______ (14) extra room in their ______ (15)

that they'd been using ______ (16) a kind of catchall ______ (17) room. They cleaned out

______ (18) room and fixed it ______ (19) and finally told Steve ______ (20) it was his. Steve

______ (21) really happy. He made ______ (22) kinds of rash promises ______ (23) he

never kept, uh, especially ______ (24) keeping it clean.

On ______ (25) first night it . . . that ______ (26) slept in his new ______ (27), there was a terrible ________(28). It was the first ________(29) that Steve had ever ________(30). It was just awful. ________(31) was flashing and the ________(32) was so loud that ________(33) house seemed to be ________(34).

After a few minutes, ________(35) parents went to his ________(36). They thought he'd be ________(37) to death in all ________(38) noise.

But Steve wasn't ________(39) at all. He was ________(40) mad. He was so ________(41) his face was red. ________(42) said, "Now I understand ________(43) you gave me this ________(44). It's so noisy here ________(45) no one else wanted ________(46)!"

SHARING ROOMS

Discussion

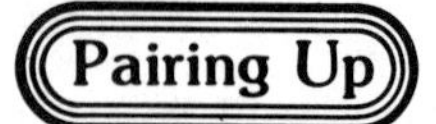

Work with another student. One of you will be **A,** and the other will be **B.** When you finish the activity, change parts and repeat it. Student **B** may answer with one of the choices, or s/he may provide his/her own response.

Private Rooms

STUDENT A: (Ask B if s/he thinks children should have their own room.)

______________________________?

STUDENT B: 1. Yes. I think it's generally good.
2. No. I don't think it's a good idea.

3. ______________________________.

STUDENT A: (Ask why s/he thinks that.)

______________________________?

STUDENT B: 1. It makes them feel independent.
2. It makes them feel insecure.

3. ______________________________.

STUDENT A: (Ask if s/he had his/her own room.)

______________________________?

STUDENT B: 1. Yes. When I started high school.
2. No. I doubled up with my *brother/sister.*

3. ______________________________.

Punishing Children

STUDENT A: (Ask B if s/he thinks parents should punish their children.)

______________________________?

STUDENT B: 1. Yes. I think it's necessary.
2. No. I don't think it's necessary.

3. ______________________________.

STUDENT A: (Ask if s/he was punished when s/he was a child.)

______________________________?

STUDENT B: 1. Yes. That's why I feel the way I do.
2. No. No one at home believed in it.

3. ______________________________.

STUDENT A: (Ask what his/her parents did.)

______________________________?

STUDENT B: 1. They spanked me.
2. They never punished me.

3. ______________________________.

Tuning In

Check to see if you know the meanings of these words from the discussion.

1. *to double up:* to share a room with another person
2. *to ignore:* to refuse to pay attention to

Summing Up

Read these statements about the discussion. Listen to the recording as many times as you like. Then choose the best answer for each of the statements, and write the letter in the space.

1. Gary had his own room ______.
   a. before his sister got married
   b. after his sister got married
   c. all of his life
   d. after he left home

2. ______ has always had a private room.
   a. Bette
   b. Gary
   c. Chuck
   d. Sharon

3. Sharon never had a room of her own when she was a child because ______.
   a. she had many brothers and sisters
   b. she never wanted one
   c. her parents refused
   d. she was afraid of the dark

4. Chuck thinks children feel ______ when they have their own room.
   a. happier
   b. lonelier
   c. more secure
   d. more independent

5. Bette thinks small children ______.
   a. should not have their own room
   b. should have their own room
   c. should be ignored
   d. should be independent

Retelling

Retell the discussion in your own words. You may use the sentences below as a guide.

The first woman (Sharon) asked the other people if they ______________________

______________________ when ______________________________.

The first man (Gary) and the second woman (Bette) ______________________

______________________, but the second man (Chuck) ______________

________________ because ________________________________.

Sharon didn't have her own room because ________________________________

________________________________.

Gary got his own room when ________________________________,

and Bette did when ________________________________.

Chuck thinks it's good for children to have their own room because ________

________________________________. Sharon

believes that ________________________________, but Bette

disagrees because ________________________________.

Drawing Out

Read the statements below. Listen to the discussion, and think about what the speakers are saying. Then decide if each statement is *possible* or *not probable* because of the information in the discussion. Find some evidence to support your answer.

1. Chuck might share things as easily as the other people in the discussion.
2. Bette would probably be a good babysitter.
3. Sharon's children will probably have their own rooms.
4. Bette would probably take her small child with her instead of hiring a babysitter.
5. Sharon would probably have a small family, that is, few children.

Filling In

Listen to the recording, and fill in the blanks. You may listen to the discussion as many times as you need to.

SHARON: Did you have your own room when you were little, Gary?

GARY: No, for I think ______ (1) first twenty years of ______ (2) life, I had somebody ______ (3) in the room with ______ (4).

SHARON: What about you, Bette?

BETTE: ______ (5) didn't when I was ______ (6) little . . . uh, up in a . . .

SHARON: ______ (7), and Chuck, you did ______ (8) you don't have any ______ (9) and sisters.

CHUCK: I've always ________ (10) my own room.

SHARON: I ________ (11) wanted my own room, ________ (12) know, because there were ________ (13) of us in the ________ (14) and we always had ________ (15) double up and stuff. ________ (16), I had my . . . my own ________ (17) the first time when ________ (18) was about twenty-five ________ (19) something.

GARY: I was very ________ (20) when my sister got ________ (21) because then I could ________ (22) her room.

SHARON: Oh, really?

GARY: And for the ________ (23) time I had my ________ (24) room, I felt very ________ (25).

SHARON: Yeah.

BETTE: I did too. ________ (26) I was . . . started to ________ (27) to high school, my ________ (28) thought it was time ________ (29) I had my own ________ (30).

SHARON: I wish my parents ________ (31) thought that, but there ________ (32) only four bedrooms in ________ (33) house for nine people ________ (34) we really were . . .

CHUCK: So ________ (35) the only one here ________ (36) really had his own ________ (37) all his life . . . but I have . . . but I don't know . . .

BETTE: What do you think that's done for you?

CHUCK: I think it's . . . I ________ (38) it's generally good. I ________ (39) whenever possible because I ________ (40) it makes people feel ________ (41) independent and maybe a . . .

BETTE: Well, do ________ (42) think even a small ________ (43) should have their own ________ (44)?

SHARON: I think so.

CHUCK: Sure, sure.

BETTE: Mmm, I don't know. What age?

SHARON: I really do. I . . . I think from ________ (45) beginning.

CHUCK: Yeah, I think ________ (46) too.

BETTE: No, I don't.

SHARON: Why?

BETTE: Well, I ________ (47), uh, I think, uh, for like ________ (48) small baby, you know, ________ (49) you're maybe at least ________ (50) year or two years ________ (51), uh, just the sense of ________ (52) that develops in a ________ (53) in . . . in the presence of ________ (54) people, you know, and ________ (55) a child's just put ________ (56) a room . . .

SHARON: Mmm . . .

CHUCK: But . . .

BETTE: . . . in a cold room with . . .

CHUCK: ________ (57) don't mean just put ________ (58) child in a cold ________ (59) and ignore him.

SHARON: I ________ (60) you probably should do ________ (61).

GARY: Ignore the child? (*laughter*)

SHARON: ________ (62), I'm just joking, of ________ (63).

Speaking Out

Read the discussion suggestions below, and choose one to talk or write about.

1. HAVING YOUR OWN ROOM: When you were a child, did you have your own room? Did your friends have their own rooms? Do you think it is good or bad for a small child to sleep alone? Why?
2. BEING INDEPENDENT: In the discussion, one of the speakers said having your own room makes you "feel more independent." Do you agree with his idea? Is being independent important for you?
3. PRIVACY: Is privacy very important to you? If you could choose, would you like to live alone or with many people? Have you ever lived alone for a long time?
4. BEING ALONE: Do you like to be alone? What do you do when you are alone?
5. SOLVING PROBLEMS: How do you solve your problems? Do you ask others for advice? What do you usually do?

UNIT TEN
THE FLIGHT ATTENDANT
Monolog

Getting Set

Listen to the recording, and write the sentences of the introduction in the lines below.

1. ______________________________ (8 words)
2. ______________________________ (8 words)
3. ______________________________ (8 words)
4. ______________________________ (5 words)

Tuning In

Check to see if you know the meanings of these words from the monolog.

1. *stewardess:* a woman who serves passengers on an airplane, usually called *flight attendant*
2. *hectic:* very busy
3. *lap:* the front part of the body (when sitting) from the waist to the knees

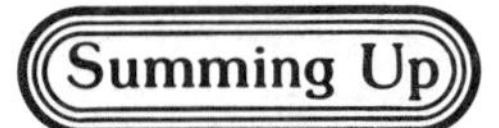

Read these five statements about the monolog. Listen to the recording as many times as you like. Then choose the best answer for each of the statements, and write the letter in the space.

1. The flight attendant was very ______.
   a. happy
   b. sad
   c. sleepy
   d. busy

2. During the flight there were many problems. One of these was ______.
   a. a small boy
   b. a sleeping gentleman
   c. trouble with the engine
   d. trouble with the movie

3. A small boy ______ the flight attendant and she almost fell on someone.
   a. threw a magazine at
   b. poured water on
   c. ran into
   d. pointed to

4. At home parents sometimes tell ______ children to go play outside.
   a. polite
   b. noisy
   c. sick
   d. shy

5. Even though the flight attendant and the little boy were on an airplane, she told him to ______.
   a. read a magazine
   b. play outside
   c. sit down
   d. be quiet

Retelling

Tell the story in your own words. You may use the sentences below as a guide.

The stewardess had a difficult time because while she ______________________________

______________________________, the plane ______________________________

______________________________. The passengers ______________________________

______________________________. A boy was ______________________________

______________________________. At one point, he ______________________________

______________________________. Then the stewardess said, ______________________________

______________________________.

Filling In

Listen to the recording, and fill in the blanks. You may listen to the monolog as many times as you need to.

The stewardess had a hectic time on a trip from one coast to the other. Uh, sh—. . . there were lots of ______ (1) pockets and the plane ______ (2) going up and down ______ (3) with all the passengers ______ (4) the plane, uh, and trying ______ (5) serve them food and ______ (6), it was just a ______ (7) bad time for her. ______ (8) compou-. . . uh, to make matters worse, uh, ______ (9) were lots of passengers ______ (10) were complaining, asking for ______ (11) and glasses of water ______ (12) aspirin and magazines and ______ (13) poor stewardess was just ______ (14) exhausted. Well, making matters ______ (15) worse, was this kid ______ (16) up and down the ______ (17) shouting and hitting people ______ (18) making all sorts of ______ (19). And at one point ______ (20) even, uh, uh, knocked the stewardess ______ (21) into the lap of a, a ______ (22) gentleman. Well, when this ______ (23), she bent down after ______ (24) a long, hard trip ______ (25) she smiled sweetly and ______ (26) in the child's ear, "______ (27) boy, why don't you ______ (28) and play outside?"

FLYING
Discussion

Pairing Up

Work with another student. One of you will be **A,** and the other will be **B.** When you finish the activity, change parts and repeat it. Student **B** may answer with one of the choices, or s/he may provide his/her own response.

A Special Fear

STUDENT A: (Ask B if there's something s/he's really afraid of.)

____?

STUDENT B: 1. Yes. I'm really afraid of _______________.
2. No. There's nothing special.

3. ____.

STUDENT A: (Ask if s/he knows why s/he feels that way.)

____?

STUDENT B: 1. Yes. It goes back to my childhood.
2. No. I've never been able to figure it out.

3. ____.

STUDENT A: (Ask if s/he's ever tried to overcome it.)

____?

STUDENT B: 1. Yes. And I did a little bit.
2. Yes. But I couldn't at all.

3. ____.

Flying Lessons

STUDENT A: (Ask B if s/he'd like to take flying lessons.)

____?

STUDENT B: 1. Yes. I'd really like to be able to fly.
2. No. I prefer staying on the ground.

3. ____.

STUDENT A: (Ask if s/he'd like to be a commercial pilot.)

____?

STUDENT B: 1. Yes. That's what I'd really like to do.
2. No. I'd just like to fly for fun.

3. ____.

STUDENT A: (Ask if s/he's ever been in a small plane.)

____?

STUDENT B: 1. Yes. And I liked it.
2. No. And I really don't want to.
3. ______________________________.

Tuning In

Check to see if you know the meanings of these words from the discussion.

1. *palm* : the lined part of your hand (under the fingers)
2. *to perspire:* to lose water from your body through your skin
3. *to overcome:* to conquer
4. *to approach:* to come near to
5. *runway:* an area with a hard surface where airplanes take off and land
6. *terrified:* very afraid
7. *to taxi:* to move very slowly on the ground before taking off or after landing

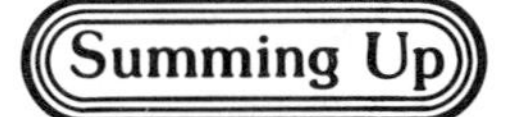

Summing Up

Read these statements about the discussion. Listen to the recording as many times as you like. Then choose the best answer for each of the statements, and write the letter in the space.

1. Chuck and Sharon ______ flying very much.
   a. avoid
   b. fear
   c. dislike
   d. like
2. Bette once took flying lessons to ______.
   a. conquer her fear of flying
   b. complete her education
   c. impress her friends
   d. get a job
3. Bette said she was ______ in overcoming her fear of flying.
   a. successful
   b. not successful
   c. impressive
   d. delighted
4. Gary is afraid of flying so he ______ when he flies.
   a. eats a lot
   b. drinks a lot
   c. takes sleeping pills
   d. takes a good book
5. Chuck and Sharon think Gary ______ flying.
   a. wants to do more
   b. expects to study more
   c. needs more hours of
   d. misses the fun of

Retelling

Retell the discussion in your own words. You may use the sentences below as a guide.

The first woman (Bette) asked the second woman (Sharon) if she ______________

____, and Sharon said ______________

____________________________. Then Bette asked if she would like to ____________

____________________________________. Sharon and the first man (Chuck) both said

that ______________________________, but the second man (Gary) ____________

____.

Bette took flying lessons because ____

____________________________________. She once flew a plane with an experienced

pilot, but she didn't ____.

When Gary takes a long trip, he ____

______________________. Sharon likes ____________________________________.

Bette likes small planes because ____.

Drawing Out

Read the statements below. Listen to the discussion, and think about what the speakers are saying. Then decide if each statement is *possible* or *not probable* because of the information in the discussion. Find some evidence to support your answer.

1. Gary might be interested in mountain climbing.
2. Gary might carry an umbrella even on a sunny day.
3. Bette might like riding a motorcycle.
4. Bette and Gary might react the same way in a frightening situation.
5. Chuck was probably serious when he asked Bette if they landed the airplane at Kaanapali.

Filling In

Listen to the recording, and fill in the blanks. You may listen to the discussion as many times as you need to.

BETTE: Sharon, do you like to fly?

SHARON: Hm, very much. It's really ________ (1) every time I get ________ (2) an airplane.

BETTE: Have you ________ (3) thought . . . have any of ________ (4) ever thought about, uh, taking ________ (5) lessons?

SHARON: Uh-huh. I'd like to, ______ (6).

CHUCK: So would I, very ______ (7).

GARY: Not me.
CHUCK: Really?
GARY: Every time I get ______ (8) a plane my . . . the ______ (9) of my hands start ______ (10) perspire.

CHUCK: Oh, I like flying.
BETTE: I do too, Gary, but . . .
CHUCK: Really, Bette?

BETTE: . . . uh, I took flying ______ (11) myself . . .

SHARON: Did you really?
BETTE: . . . simply because I was so . . .
SHARON: When?

BETTE: . . . ______ (12). Um, the last, well, maybe ______ (13) two years ago I ______ (14) a ground . . . ground pilot. ______ (15) then I have a ______ (16) of friends who fly.

CHUCK: How many hours was that . . . of ______ (17)?

BETTE: Well, ground ______ (18) is like, is only, ______ (19) don't know, it's a ______ (20). It was an evening ______ (21) at the university, huh? To ______ (22) you for your written ______ (23). And then I have a ______ (24) of friends who fly ______ (25) planes, so . . .
CHUCK: Did you ever fly?

BETTE: Yeah. ______ (26) you know, with an ______ (27) pilot in the seat.

GARY: ______ (28) you overcome your fear ______ (29) heights in flying?

BETTE: Oh, nooo. It was even ______ (30) because I knew . . . (*laughter*) I ______ (31) just enough to . . . to, uh, ______ (32) frightened but not to ______ (33) exactly what to do, ______ (34) know, and one time . . .

SHARON: Mm.

BETTE: . . . ______ (35) were flying into Kaanapali.

SHARON: Hah.

BETTE: ________ the plane . . . we made ________ six approaches. And everybody
36 37

________ out on the runway ________ bets on whether we ________ going to land
38 39 40

or not. I was terrified! I was really terrified.

CHUCK: Did you land?

BETTE: Yes, we did. (*laughter*)

GARY: Whenever I go on ________ long, long trip by ________, I take sleeping pills
41 42

________ I'll sleep.
43

SHARON: Oh, Gary, ________ . . . you miss all the fun.
44

CHUCK: Yeah, that's ________ I think, Sharon, 'cause I really like . . .
45

SHARON: You know, every time ________ plane taxis and the ________ it leaves the
46 47

ground, ________ think it's like a ________.
48 49

CHUCK: Yeah.

SHARON: I mean, I, my, my, my whole ________ is just filled with ________.
50 51

GARY: I think it's like ________ miracle and I don't ________ it's going to make it.
52 53

(*laughter*) That's why I take sleeping pills.

SHARON: Oh, I love it.

BETTE: Oh, it's also, too . . . especially in a small ________, you're really close to
54

________.
55

Speaking Out

Read the discussion suggestions below, and choose one to talk or write about.

1. FLYING: Have you ever flown in an airplane? Do you like to fly? Have you ever had any bad experiences while flying? Would you like to learn how to fly a plane? Why or why not?
2. TAKING TRIPS: What is the longest trip you've ever taken? Where did you go? How did you get there? What did you do there? Did you have any special reasons for going?
3. CHILDREN IN PUBLIC: How do you feel about children who misbehave in public places? Would you say something to a child who was misbehaving?
4. BEING CLOSE TO NATURE: Is it important for you to feel close to nature? What kinds of things can you do to help you feel that way? How often do you do those things?
5. BEING FRIGHTENED: What kinds of things really scare you? Flying? Driving fast? Deep water? Why do you think you are afraid?

UNIT ELEVEN
THE SOUR SOUP
Monolog

Getting Set

Listen to the recording, and write the sentences of the introduction in the lines below.

1. ______________________________ (6 words)
2. ______________________________ (8 words)
3. ______________________________ (7 words)
4. ______________________________ (7 words)

Tuning In

Check to see if you know the meanings of these words from the monolog.

1. *reasonable:* logical
2. *vinegar:* a sour liquid used to flavor food

Read these five statements about the monolog. Listen to the monolog as many times as you like. Then choose the best answer for each of the statements, and write the letter in the space.

1. Sharon thinks traveling is ______.
   a. expensive
   b. unusual
   c. a good experience
   d. a waste of time
2. Sharon was ______ in a restaurant when this incident took place.
   a. eating a salad
   b. having a sandwich
   c. reading a book
   d. drinking coffee
3. Two people came into the restaurant who ______.
   a. could speak the local language
   b. couldn't speak the local language
   c. knew Sharon
   d. knew the waiter
4. They ordered their food by ______.
   a. asking the waiter for advice
   b. asking Sharon for advice
   c. pointing at some pictures in the menu
   d. pointing at Sharon's food
5. The two people drank the sauce because ______.
   a. it was on a special plate
   b. it was in a small bowl
   c. of the color
   d. of the taste

Retelling

Tell the story in your own words. You may use the sentences below as a guide.

Sharon enjoys ______________________________.

Once when she was sitting in a restaurant, she watched ______________________________

______________________________. They didn't ______________________________

______________________________, so they ordered by ______________________________.

The waiter didn't ______________________________.

When he returned, he brought them ______________________________.

The two people ______________________________, but they soon

found out that ______________________________.

Filling In

Listen to the recording, and fill in the blanks. You may listen to the monolog as many times as you need to.

A lot of people travel to foreign countries in the summertime and it's really a good experience. I've done a lot ______ (1) that myself and I've ______ (2) a lot of interesting ______ (3) when I've traveled.

One ______ (4) I was sitting in ______ (5) restaurant watching the people ______ (6) in and out, just ______ (7) some coffee, and kind ______ (8) enjoying the experience of ______ (9) in another place. I ______ (10) at one point two ______ (11) come in and sit ______ (12) at a table. They ______ (13) quite know what to ______ (14) and they didn't speak ______ (15) language at all, but ______ (16) were pictures in the ______ (17) and they thought, well, ______ (18) could probably get by ______ (19) pointing at things so ______ (20) pointed at something and ______ (21) waiter seemed to think ______ (22) was reasonable because he ______ (23) ask any questions. So ______ (24) brought what they were ______ (25) to eat. In doing ______ (26), he brought the sauce ______ (27) the

meat that they ________ going to eat first ________ put it on the ________. The two
28 29 30

people who ________ eating didn't understand what ________ ordered so they didn't
31 32

________ what he'd brought. They ________ at it and since ________ was in a small
33 34 35

________, they thought, "Well, this ________ be the soup," and ________ drank it.
36 37 38

You can ________ their surprise to find ________ that it was almost ________
39 40 41

hundred percent vinegar!

CLEANING HOUSE

Discussion

Pairing Up

Work with another student. One of you will be **A,** and the other will be **B.** When you finish the activity, change parts and repeat it. Student **B** may answer with one of the choices, or s/he may provide his/her own response.

Cleaning

STUDENT A: (Ask B if it's important for his/her *apartment/house/room* to be clean.)

____?

STUDENT B: 1. Yes. I have a thing about a clean place.
2. No. I don't think it's very important.

3. ____.

STUDENT A: (Ask if s/he often cleans his/her place.)

____?

STUDENT B: 1. Once or twice a week.
2. Only once or twice a month.

3. ____.

STUDENT A: (Ask if s/he thinks that's too often or not often enough.)

____?

STUDENT B: 1. Well, maybe it's a little exaggerated.
2. No, I don't think so.

3. ____.

Fast Food Restaurants

STUDENT A: (Ask B if s/he likes fast food places.)

____?

STUDENT B: 1. Sure. I really like hamburgers.
2. Not very much. I always feel I haven't really eaten.

3. ____.

STUDENT A: (Ask if fast food places are popular in his/her country.)

____?

STUDENT B: 1. Yes. They've really caught on.
2. Not really. People aren't used to them.

3. ____.

STUDENT A: (Ask what his/her favorite fast food restaurant is.)

____?

STUDENT B: 1. ____________. They have really good (*pizza*).
2. I guess I don't have one.
3. ____.

Tuning In

Check to see if you know the meanings of these words from the discussion.

1. *underneath:* under
2. *stain:* an unwanted spot (such as coffee on your clothes)
3. *to wipe:* to rub with cloth or paper in order to clean or dry
4. *to spill:* to cause to fall out of a container
5. *fastidious:* careful in all details
6. *compulsion:* a force inside you that you can't control
7. *neurotic:* abnormally anxious

Read these statements about the discussion. Listen to the recording as many times as you like. Then choose the best answer for each of the statements, and write the letter in the space.

1. Chuck sometimes ______ when he eats breakfast.
   a. makes coffee c. listens to the radio
   b. spills coffee d. reads the newspaper
2. Gary feels a clean house is ______.
   a. difficult to have c. not so important
   b. difficult to enjoy d. very important
3. Having a clean room is more important to ______ now than it was before.
   a. Bette c. Gary
   b. Chuck d. Sharon
4. Chuck thinks being ______ is more important than having a clean house.
   a. different c. comfortable
   b. neurotic d. compulsive
5. Bette sometimes feels strongly that she ______ housecleaning.
   a. doesn't do a good job c. doesn't need to do
   b. does a good job d. needs to do

Retelling

Retell the discussion in your own words. You may use the sentences below as a guide.

The first man (Gary) complained that the second man (Chuck) ______________

____.

The first woman (Sharon) didn't use to ________________________________,

but now ____.

Chuck doesn't think ____,

and the second woman (Bette) agrees with him. Sharon believes that the need to clean

depends on ____.

Bette sometimes ____,

but Chuck never feels that way.

Read the statements below. Listen to the discussion, and think about what the speakers are saying. Then decide if each statement is *possible* or *not probable* because of information in the discussion. Find some evidence to support your answer.

1. Bette probably laughed about Chuck spilling coffee because she would expect him to do that kind of thing.
2. Gary might clean his desk every day after he used it.
3. Sharon might watch television whether her roommate liked it or not.
4. Sharon probably wanted to talk about her own experiences when she asked Gary if he'd always been so clean.
5. Chuck probably thinks Gary and Bette's attitudes are silly.

Filling In

Listen to the recording, and fill in the blanks. You may listen to the discussion as many times as you need to.

GARY: You know, the other day af— . . . after Chuck left, I looked and the space underneath the table where he was sitting eating breakfast and I found some coffee stains. So, I wiped them ________ (1) and, uh, then, the next ________ (2) . . .

BETTE: You found some more. (*laughter*)

GARY: In the very same place.

SHARON: Really?

GARY: Yeah.

CHUCK: Well, what's wrong with that? I enjoy my coffee. If I spill a little bit, . . .

GARY: It's crazy. I, I, I, I have this ________ (3) about a clean place, ________ (4) know.

SHARON: Have you always ________ (5) like that, Gary?

BETTE: Very ________ (6).

GARY: Not . . . not . . .

SHARON: You know, when I was in ________ (7), I hardly ever made ________ (8) bed or cleaned my ________ (9). I really didn't at ________ (10) . . .

GARY: Uh-huh.

SHARON: . . . and my first roommate ________ (11) Honolulu . . . I never cleaned ________ (12) apartment and now I ________ (13) every day make my ________ (14), every day clean the ________ (15) and every day keep things neat.

CHUCK: Sharon, do you do ________ (16) because you want to ________ (17) because you feel you ________ (18) to?

BETTE: Is it a compulsion?

SHARON: No, because . . . no, because I really ________ (19) to.

CHUCK: Really?

SHARON: Yeah. But I think ________ (20) become kind of habit ________ (21).

CHUCK: I don't think it's so ________ (22) if you're comfortable. I ________ (23) think it makes so ________ (24) difference.

BETTE: That's true. That's true.

SHARON: It depends on ________ (25) many other people you ________ (26).

CHUCK: Well . . . of course.

GARY: It depends on what kind of animal you are, you know. It's like a pig. ________ (27) with a pig.

BETTE: Oh, it is not, Gary!

SHARON: No, Gary. Not really.

CHUCK: Oh, Gary.

BETTE: It's not, Gary. It's just that somebody . . . I . . . I am at sometimes ______ [28],
neurotically . . . ah, uh, you know . . .

GARY: Yeah. (*laughter*)

BETTE: . . . in a clean . . .

GARY: You want to clean things.

BETTE: Housecleaning! Yeah, I just have to.

GARY: Yeah. Yeah. Yeah . . . I feel the same way.

CHUCK: Fortunately, I ______ [29] feel that way.

BETTE: And sometimes . . . sometimes . . .

SHARON: Unfortunately, you never feel that way. (*laughter*)

CHUCK: But I just don't ______ [30] it's so important. Sometimes, ______ [31].

BETTE: That's true. There're a ______ [32] more important things to ______ [33].

CHUCK: Mmm.

Speaking Out

Read the discussion suggestions below, and choose one to talk or write about.

1. CLEANING: Is it important to you to live in a clean place? Why? How often do you clean your room/apartment/house? Do you think it's different when you don't live alone? Would having a roommate affect your feelings about a clean place? Why?
2. HOUSEHOLD DUTIES: Do you think children should help out at home? Will you (or do you) give your children their own household duties? Why?
3. BREAKFAST: Do you usually eat breakfast? What kind of things do you eat for breakfast? Is breakfast an important meal for you?
4. HAVING A COMPULSION: Is there something that you are compulsive about? Being clean? Combing your hair? Sleeping with the window open? What causes people to have compulsions?
5. ROOMMATES: Do you have a roommate now, or have you ever had one? How do you (or did you) get along? What are the good and bad things about having a roommate?

UNIT TWELVE
THE ANECDOTE
Monolog

Getting Set

Listen to the recording, and write the sentences of the introduction in the lines below.

1. ______________________________ (10 words)
2. ______________________________ (9 words)
3. ______________________________ (8 words)
4. ______________________________ (6 words)

Check to see if you know the meanings of these words from the monolog.

1. *to encourage:* to give confidence to someone
2. *anecdote:* a short, funny story
3. *tale:* a story

Read these five statements about the monolog. Listen to the recording as many times as you like. Then choose the best answer for each of the statements, and write the letter in the space.

1. Steve was ______ a good student.
   a. always
   b. never
   c. sometimes
   d. hardly ever
2. A student told about a politician who was good at ______.
   a. giving reports
   b. getting votes
   c. remembering names
   d. telling stories
3. The student told Steve the meaning of the word ______.
   a. *tail*
   b. *politician*
   c. *anecdote*
   d. *puppy*
4. The teacher told Steve to use *anecdote* in ______.
   a. his homework
   b. his report
   c. a definition
   d. a sentence
5. Steve made a strange sentence because he ______.
   a. confused *tale* and *tail*
   b. was a good student
   c. wanted to show off
   d. liked animals

Retelling

Tell the story in your own words. You may use the sentences below as a guide.

Chuck's cousin Steve wasn't a good ______________________________.

The teachers always wanted the students to ______________________________

______________________________. One day the class was ______________________________

______________________________. One student read to the class about ______________________________

______________________________. Steve didn't ______________________________

______________, so he ______________________________. The

other student told him that ______________________________.

Then the teacher asked Steve to ______________________________.

At last, Steve said ______________________________

______________________________.

Filling In

Listen to the recording, and fill in the blanks. You may listen to the monolog as many times as you need to.

My cousin Steve has never been what you would call a good student. The family tells a ______ (1) about Steve when he ______ (2), uh, in grade school. Uh, at ______ (3) time the teachers encouraged ______ (4) students to read a ______ (5) and tried to always ______ (6) them to learn to ______ (7) new words. Sometimes the ______ (8) were successful and sometimes ______ (9) weren't. Often with Steve ______ (10) weren't.

One day in ______ (11) they were giving reports ______ (12) newspapers. One student read ______ (13) the class about a ______ (14) who was very good ______ (15), uh, anecdotes.

Steve didn't understand ______ (16) meaning of *anecdote*, so ______ (17) asked the student, "What ______ (18) *anecdote* mean?"

The student, ________ [19] was probably, uh, very happy ________ [20] show off, told Steve ________ [21] it meant "story" or ________ [22].

Of course the teacher ________ [23] listening and she told ________ [24] to try to make ________ [25] sentence with *anecdote* in ________ [26]. Steve thought and thought, ________ [27] he didn't say anything.

________ [28] teacher said, "Oh, Steve, ________ [29] easy. You just heard ________ [30] an anecdote is a ________ [31]."

Finally Steve said, "Last ________ [32] my dog Spot had ________ [33] puppies. After a few ________ [34] my dad cut off ________ [35] their anecdotes."

NURSERY SCHOOLS

Discussion

Work with another student. One of you will be **A,** and the other will be **B.** When you finish the activity, change parts and repeat it. Student **B** may answer with one of the choices, or s/he may provide his/her own response.

Nursery Schools

STUDENT A: (Ask B what s/he thinks of nursery school.)

______________________________?

STUDENT B: 1. I think it's kind of a good idea.
2. I don't think it's such a good idea.
3. ______________________________.

STUDENT A: (Ask why s/he thinks so.)

______________________________?

STUDENT B: 1. It's good to begin socializing then.
2. It's too early to begin socializing.
3. ______________________________.

STUDENT A: (Ask what kind of nursery school s/he thinks is best.)

______________________________?

STUDENT B: 1. One that's fairly formal.
2. One that's just a play situation.
3. ______________________________.

New Words

STUDENT A: (Ask B how s/he learns new words in English.)

______________________________?

STUDENT B: 1. I try to listen to what people say.
2. I try to read a lot.
3. ______________________________.

STUDENT A: (Ask if s/he thinks knowing a lot of words is helpful.)

______________________________?

STUDENT B: 1. Sure. Otherwise you can't understand anything.
2. Not unless you know them well.
3. ______________________________.

STUDENT A: (Ask how s/he practices using new words.)

______________________________?

STUDENT B: 1. I use them in conversation.
2. I use them when I write.

3. ______________________________.

Tuning In

Check to see if you know the meanings of these words from the discussion.

1. *folks:* people (informal)
2. *to repress:* to keep feelings and ideas in your mind instead of showing them
3. *to socialize :* to take part in activities with other people

Read these statements about the discussion. Listen to the recording as many times as you like. Then choose the best answer for each of the statements, and write the letter in the space.

1. Sharon is in favor of nursery schools if they are ______.
   a. different from ordinary schools
   b. preparation for ordinary schools
   c. the same as ordinary schools
   d. better than ordinary schools
2. Bette and Chuck feel schools ______ over the way students think.
   a. should have more control
   b. need a lot of control
   c. have very little control
   d. have too much control
3. Chuck thinks nursery schools should help children ______.
   a. become serious students
   b. become more creative
   c. become better readers
   d. become more sociable
4. Gary thinks nursery school is ______ for children to mix with other children.
   a. not the only place
   b. the only place
   c. not the easiest place
   d. the easiest place
5. Bette feels children ______ with people outside of their own families until the age of five or six.
   a. never mix
   b. always mix
   c. aren't ready to mix
   d. are ready to mix

Retelling

Retell the discussion in your own words. You may use the sentences below as a guide.

The first woman (Bette) asked the other people for their opinions about ______________________________. The second woman (Sharon) thinks ______________

____. The first man (Gary)

says that it depends on ________________________. The second man

(Chuck) adds that it also depends on ________________________

____. Bette wonders

whether ________________________________because she believes

that our educational system is ________________________________.

Chuck asks Bette if she thinks it is possible to ________________________

____.

Bette doesn't believe that children are ready ________________________

____. Gary agrees, but adds that

____.

Drawing Out

Read the statements below. Listen to the discussion, and think about what the speakers are saying. Then decide if each statement is *possible* or *not probable* because of the information in the discussion. Find some evidence to support your answer.

1. Sharon might think it's good to have more centers that take care of the children of working parents.
2. Gary might encourage his children to play with other children.
3. Chuck might send his children to a summer music camp.
4. Bette might have a birthday party for her three-year-old child and invite other children to attend.
5. Gary might have definite opinions about what children should learn in school.

Filling In

Listen to the recording, and fill in the blanks. You may listen to the discussion as many times as you need to.

BETTE: What do you folks think of sending three-year-olds to nursery school?

SHARON: I think it's kind ________ (1) a good idea. Tamon's ________ (2) girl goes to nursery ________ (3), and she likes it ________ (4) much.

BETTE: Why do you ________ (5) it's a good idea?

SHARON: ________ (6) she's an only child ________ (7) the moment and her ________ (8) has to take care ________ (9) her and she enjoys ________ (10) around other people her ________ (11), I mean, little kids.

GARY: ________ (12) think it depends on ________ (13) the child learns in ________ (14) nursery school. What sort ________ (15) thing are you talking ________ (16), Bette? What kind . . .

BETTE: I was ________ (17) of a fairly formal ________ (18), you know, like the ________ (19) Start programs where you're ________ (20) a person to go ________ (21) kindergarten or the first ________ (22).

GARY: Well, teaching them what? ________ (23)?

BETTE: Yeah, yeah, not just ________ (24) play situation.

CHUCK: I think ________ (25) depends very much on ________ (26) family's situation and that ________ (27) child.

SHARON: Yeah, I think ________ (28). And I think even ________ (29) it's not a play ________ (30), it's not a bad ________ (31).

CHUCK: Mmm, by play situation, you . . .

BETTE: You don't think that ________ (32) you start structuring a ________ (33), you know, too much, ________ (34) soon? I mean, I ________ (35) our educational system is ________ (36) structured and very repressive . . . ________ (37) just starting the process ________ (38) couple of years earlier ________ (39) you . . .

SHARON: Well, if it's ________ (40) of the same thing, ________ (41) agree, I think.

CHUCK: But, Bette, ________ (42) it be possible, uh, to ________ (43) of start some sort ________ (44) creative thing earlier? Would ________ (45) be in favor of ________ (46)?

GARY: You mean like art? ________ (47) things like that?

SHARON: Mmm, even like reading's creative . . .

CHUCK: Well, Bette, says that ________ (48) is . . . is repressive and I ________ (49) and I'm wondering if ________ (50) could be not repressive ________ (51).

BETTE: Well, I'm also thinking, ________ (52), about what age a ________ (53) starts to socialize and ________ (54) don't think they're ready ________ (55) socializing outside of the ________ (56), you know, before the ________ (57) of about five or ________ (58).

GARY: Yeah, I agree with you.

CHUCK: Oh, really?

GARY: ________ (59) are other ways of ________ (60), uh . . . uh, with other children than ________ (61) your child off to ________ (62) nursery school.

Speaking Out

Read the discussion suggestions below, and choose one to talk or write about.

1. NURSERY SCHOOLS: How do you feel about nursery schools? What is the purpose of nursery schools? Do you think nursery schools should prepare children for school? Why?
2. BEING A FATHER: People often forget about the father when they talk about taking care of children. Do you think the father should spend the same amount of time as the mother in raising children? Why?
3. CHILDREN'S RIGHTS: Do you think of children as people with ideas and feelings? How do people from different countries treat children?
4. STRICT TEACHERS: Which do you like better, strict teachers and classes, or teachers who are not strict at all? Explain why.

Answer Key

UNIT ONE

Getting Set

1. Surprise parties are hard to do well.
2. Many things can easily go wrong.
3. The party in this story started early.
4. Somebody hid in the wrong place.

Summing Up

1. c 2. a 3. d 4. b 5. a

Pairing Up

Student A: Do you like to give gifts?
What kind of gifts do you like to give?
Do you like to give gifts any time?

Does happiness depend on money?
How long have you felt that way?
Could money help make someone a better person?

Summing Up

1. d 2. d 3. b 4. a 5. c

Drawing Out

1. Possible (Discussion line 6)
2. Possible (Discussion lines 20 and 21)
3. Not Probable (Discussion line 24)
4. Possible (Discussion line 8)
5. Possible (Discussion line 23 + embarrassed laughter)

UNIT TWO

Getting Set

1. Waiting to make a phone call can be frustrating.
2. Especially if the call is important.
3. Gary tells about waiting a long time for a phone.
4. And the reason he waits is unusual.

Summing Up

1. c 2. b 3. d 4. c 5. a

Pairing Up

Student A: Does waiting a long time bother you?
How do you feel when you have to wait?
Does it help to get impatient?

Do you use the telephone often?
What do you usually use the phone for?
Do you talk a long time on the phone?

Summing Up

1. a 2. d 3. d 4. c 5. b

Drawing Out

1. Possible (Discussion line 4)
2. Possible (Discussion lines 6 and 8)
3. Possible (Discussion line 23)
4. Not Probable (Discussion lines 8 and 22—Surprise and unbelieving intonation.)
5. Possible (Discussion lines 3 and 4)

UNIT THREE

Getting Set

1. Is your English comprehensible to other people?
2. If it's incomprehensible, it's probably a problem.
3. In this story a movie director has exactly that problem.
4. It was really hard for people to understand him.

Summing Up

1. d 2. c 3. b 4. c 5. d

Pairing Up

Student A: What kind of job would you like to have?
How important is salary?
Do you like a lot of rules?

What's your biggest problem in English?
Why do you think it's a problem?
What's your strongest point?

Summing Up

1. c 2. b 3. d 4. d 5. c

Drawing Out

1. Possible (Discussion lines 21 and 23)
2. Possible (Discussion lines 12 and 17)
3. Possible (Discussion line 13)
4. Not Probable (Discussion lines 3, 8 and 10)
5. Possible (Discussion line 49)

UNIT FOUR

Getting Set

1. When you buy something, you expect it to last.
2. If there's trouble, you ought to be able to take it back.
3. Sometimes that's easier said than done.
4. Have you ever had that happen to you?

Summing Up

1. b 2. a 3. d 4. d 5. c

Pairing Up

Student A: Do you get angry often?
What do you do when you're angry?
Is that a good way of coping with it?

How do you feel about keeping pets?
Have you ever had a pet of your own?
Which animals do you think make the best pets?

Summing Up

1. b 2. d 3. c 4. b 5. a

Drawing Out

1. Possible (Discussion lines 11 and 13)
2. Possible (Discussion line 24)
3. Possible (Discussion line 16)
4. Not Probable (Discussion line 2—Emphatic delivery of first part.)
5. Not Probable (Discussion line 15)

UNIT FIVE

Getting Set

1. Getting older's an important part of life.
2. It's something that everyone goes through.
3. You can see it when it happens to others.
4. But it's harder to see it in yourself.

Summing Up

1. d 2. b 3. a 4. c 5. c

Pairing Up

Student A: How do you feel about nudity in art?
Do you feel strange looking at nude art?
Would you paint nudes if you were an artist?

What are your feelings on censorship?
Is there censorship in your country?
Who do you think should decide what should be censored?

Summing Up

1. a 2. c 3. d 4. d 5. b

Drawing Out

1. Possible (Discussion line 4)
2. Possible (Discussion line 10)
3. Not Probable (Discussion line 29)
4. Possible (Discussion line 23)
5. Possible (Discussion line 16)

UNIT SIX

Getting Set

1. A disc jockey wanted to know how cold it was.
2. So he asked his listeners to phone the information in.
3. You'd think it'd be easy to check the temperature.
4. But actually it's harder than you'd imagine.

Summing Up

1. a 2. c 3. a 4. b 5. a

Pairing Up

Student A: Do you try to keep up with world events?
How do you know what's going on?
Do you feel you have to keep up?

Are you a responsible person?
Do you want to contribute to society?
Do you have to be informed to do that?

Summing Up

1. b 2. d 3. b 4. d 5. c

Drawing Out

1. Possible (Discussion line 1)
2. Possible (Discussion lines 2 and 9)
3. Possible (Total discussion—Sentence length, vocabulary choice and speed.)
4. Possible (Discussion lines 13 and 14)
5. Not Probable (Discussion lines 15 and 18)

UNIT SEVEN

Getting Set

1. Kids get tired of sharing their toys.
2. Especially if they've done it all their lives.
3. It isn't being stingy to feel that way.
4. Kids need some things to call their own.

Summing Up

1. a 2. b 3. c 4. d 5. d

Pairing Up

Student A: Do you have friends who are stingy?
Do you know what makes people stingy?
Do you think you're a stingy person?

Do you have any brothers and sisters?
How was that when you were growing up?
How about now?

Summing Up

1. c 2. b 3. d 4. b 5. c

Drawing Out

1. Possible (Discussion line 8)
2. Not Probable (Discussion line 14)
3. Possible (Discussion line 11)
4. Possible (Discussion line 19—No example, silence.)
5. Not Probable (Discussion lines 1 and 7—Manner of telling story, recognition of generosity.)

UNIT EIGHT

Getting Set

1. What would happen if you parked your car in a no-parking zone?
2. Probably the police'd give you a ticket.
3. Maybe they'd even tow your car away.
4. A judge has that happen in this next story.

Summing Up

1. a 2. d 3. b 4. c 5. a

Pairing Up

Student A: Do we depend on medicine too much?
Could we get by without some of it?
How often do you use medicine?

Are the drug laws strict in your country?
Do you think that's good?
Who do you think should decide about drugs?

Summing Up

1. b 2. a 3. d 4. d 5. b

Drawing Out

1. Possible (Discussion line 8)
2. Not Probable (Discussion line 6)
3. Not Probable (Discussion line 14—He implies only a doctor can choose certain medicine.)
4. Possible (Discussion line 12)
5. Possible (Discussion line 14)

UNIT NINE

Getting Set

1. It's usually nice to have your own room.
2. It's also nice when somebody gives you something.
3. Would you want to be given something that nobody else wants?
4. Probably not, even if it's a private room.

Summing Up

1. a 2. d 3. a 4. c 5. b

Pairing Up

Student A: Do you think children should have their own room?
Why do you think that?
Did you have your own room?

Do you think parents should punish their children?
Were you punished when you were a child?
What did your parents do?

Summing Up

1. b 2. c 3. a 4. d 5. a

Drawing Out

1. Not Probable (Discussion lines 5 and 6)
2. Possible (Discussion line 25)
3. Possible (Discussion line 18)
4. Possible (Discussion line 25)
5. Possible (Discussion lines 7 and 13)

UNIT TEN

Getting Set

1. Would you want to be a flight attendant?
2. It sounds exciting, but it's really hard work.
3. Keeping people happy is part of that work.
4. Dealing with kids is too.

Summing Up

1. d 2. a 3. c 4. b 5. b

Pairing Up

Student A: Is there something you're really afraid of?
Do you know why you feel that way?
Have you ever tried to overcome it?

Would you like to take flying lessons?
Would you like to be a commercial pilot?
Have you ever been in a small plane?

Summing Up

1. d 2. a 3. b 4. c 5. d

Drawing Out

1. Not Probable (Discussion lines 8 and 21)
2. Possible (Discussion line 35)
3. Possible (Discussion line 37)
4. Not Probable (Discussion lines 10–16 and 29)
5. Not Probable (Discussion lines 26–28)

UNIT ELEVEN

Getting Set

1. Traveling can be a good experience.
2. And part of that's trying new food.
3. But how do you know what to order?
4. Maybe it's better to ask for help.

Summing Up

1. c 2. d 3. b 4. c 5. b

Pairing Up

Student A: Is it important for your apartment/house/room to be clean?
Do you often clean your place?
Do you think that's too often or not often enough?

Do you like fast food places?
Are fast food places popular in your country?
What's your favorite fast food restaurant?

Summing Up

1. b 2. d 3. d 4. c 5. d

Drawing Out

1. Possible (Discussion line 2)
2. Possible (Discussion line 7)
3. Not Probable (Discussion line 21)
4. Possible (Discussion line 8)
5. Possible (Discussion line 33)

UNIT TWELVE

Getting Set

1. Using new words is a good way to learn them.
2. Teachers tell students to use them in a sentence.
3. Mistakes are made, but that's part of learning.
4. Sometimes the mistakes are really funny.

Summing Up

1. b 2. d 3. c 4. d 5. a

Pairing Up

Student A: What do you think of nursery school?
Why do you think so?
What kind of nursery school do you think is best?

How do you learn new words in English?
Do you think knowing a lot of words is helpful?
How do you practice using new words?

Summing Up

1. a 2. d 3. b 4. a 5. c

Drawing Out

1. Possible (Discussion line 4)
2. Possible (Discussion line 21)
3. Possible (Discussion line 14)
4. Not Probable (Discussion line 18)
5. Possible (Discussion line 5)

Tapescript

UNIT ONE

Monolog (CHUCK)

If you know me very well, you know I don't like birthday parties. At least, I don't like birthday parties given for, uh, me. I enjoy them when they're for other people, but when they're for me, I just don't like them.

I remember one birthday party some friends of mine had for me when I was a student at the university. Of course, I, uh, had told my roommate that I didn't want a party and I made him promise he wouldn't do anything. He agreed and I should've known better than to trust him.

On the day of my birthday, we got home from school at about, oh, I don't know, three or three-thirty. We went inside and as usual I headed for the bathroom. I went inside and started to close the door when suddenly from behind the shower curtain, a kind of desperate-sounding female voice started singing, "Happy birthday to you, happy birthday to you."

And then from all over the apartment, people joined in. There were about fifteen people hiding everywhere in the apartment. They had gotten my roommate's key and gone in earlier. They had all planned to come out of hiding just at the same time while singing. I guess I really upset their plans by going in just to wash my hands.

Discussion

1. CHUCK: You know, I really don't like having to give gifts on like Christmases and birthdays and stuff, but I like giving gifts very much on times when I just feel like doing it.
2. SHARON: I do too. And I give gifts to a lot of people that way. I, uh, maybe I like giving gifts at Christmas too, but not so much as an adult. When I was little, I did.
3. BETTE: Well, what kind of gifts do you like to give, Sharon?
4. SHARON: Almost anything. I mean, sometimes, uh, gum or cigarettes or . . . (*laughter*)
5. GARY: You give gum?
6. BETTE: You really go all out, don't you? (*laughter*)
7. SHARON: Well, no, but what I mean is, you know, if I walk by a store and I see a kind of foreign cigarettes and I know somebody likes them and doesn't usually buy them for themselves, I, you know, I might pick up a pack and give them to somebody.
8. CHUCK: Yeah, that's nice.
9. GARY: When do you give . . .
10. BETTE: How about you, Gary?
11. GARY: When you . . . when do you . . . sorry . . . when do you give packages of gum? (*laughter*)
12. SHARON: Well, just recently, my mother's been here and she likes to chew gum and I don't usually buy it, but when I see it now, you know, I might stop and just give her a pack of gum.
13. GARY: Mmm.
14. SHARON: Just for fun.
15. GARY: I like to give gifts.
16. SHARON: Yeah, I know you do.
17. BETTE: You want to give me one? (*laughter*)
18. GARY: Well, it's not your birthday, is it?
19. CHUCK: Do you . . . Gary, do you like to give, do you like giving gifts any time or just at certain times?
20. GARY: Yeah, I was going to say, uh, it's not Bette's birthday and I like to give gifts at appropriate occasions. I differ with you on that. At Christmas and birthdays, anniversaries and things like that, I like to give gifts.
21. BETTE: You're rather formalistic, then?
22. GARY: Very much so that way.
23. SHARON: But I think you have . . . much better memory than the rest of us. I think one reason I like to give gifts all the time is 'cause I re-, never remember the appropriate times.
24. GARY: Well, you have to have a system of re-, recording.
25. CHUCK: Yeah, I have that problem also.
26. SHARON: Yeah. Yeah, I, 'cause I have so many brothers and sisters and other people, I don't remember birthdays and stuff.
27. CHUCK: You can write it down.

UNIT TWO

Monolog (GARY)

Last time I was at a plane, uh, an airport, I, uh, was between planes and I had to make an important phone call and I looked around . . . all the phones that I could see were busy. So I waited in line and waited and waited. And finally, uh, the person who was talking on the phone that I was waiting for . . . waiting to use, uh, I . . . I . . . I began to listen to his conversation.

It was kind of funny because he was an old man and he was talking to his wife and he was talking about his trip. And he said, uh, that he, uh, he was having a good time and he talked about the weather and he asked about the weather back there. And all the time he was talking, uh, to his wife . . . I guess it was to his wife, but while he was talking to his wife, he . . . he was eating a sandwich and, uh, drinking coffee.

And this went on and on and on, and I really was getting impatient because this phone call I had to make was important. And, uh, maybe I waited there . . . oh, ten, fifteen, twenty minutes. And finally the guy hung up and he turned around because he . . . he had seen me standing there, and he said, "Well, I'm sorry, uh, that I took so long on the phone, but I was having dinner with my wife."

Discussion

1. GARY: I really got disgusted this morning.
2. SHARON: Why, Gary?
3. GARY: Well, we were waiting for a taxi to come here and none came.
4. SHARON: Oh, I hate to wait like that, you know.
5. GARY: I do too.
6. BETTE: Well, yeah, but sometimes you . . . you . . . what can you do about it, you know?
7. SHARON: Well, I'd rather . . .
8. CHUCK: I don't mind waiting so much.
9. SHARON: Really? I'm . . . I'm a really impatient person when I'm waiting for people.
10. CHUCK: Really, Sharon?
11. SHARON: Yeah. Or waiting for things like taxis.
12. CHUCK: How about if you have an appointment with somebody and they're a few minutes late? Does that bother you very much?
13. SHARON: If I know they're going to be late, not so much, although inside I still feel, mmm, very, mmm, strange because I don't like to wait basically.
14. CHUCK: Really?
15. BETTE: You know, I used to have this friend who hated to wait in li- . . . in lines and I think this is probably something cultural, but whenever we would go someplace like to a theater and there'd be a long line, he would run up to the very front, and just . . . just right in front of everybody buy his tickets.
16. SHARON: Oh, I don't like that.
17. CHUCK: So you always got in very fast.
18. BETTE: Of course we did, but, you know, I . . . I . . .
19. SHARON: Weren't you embarrassed by that?
20. BETTE: I . . . yeees . . . yes.
21. SHARON: I . . . I don't know, you know, when I go home from school at night, I go home with Kathy. And frequently she talks to her students after class and I really get impatient waiting 'cause we miss the train if she doesn't hurry.
22. CHUCK: Well, that's a different . . . I can understand getting impatient in that situation because . . . you'd miss your train. But if you're just sort of waiting in line or waiting in a bank or something . . . I don't . . . I don't think it's . . . helps to get impatient.
23. GARY: How do you feel when you wait for the same person and that person's always late? Over and over and . . .
24. BETTE: I just leave without them.
25. SHARON: Really?
26. BETTE: (*laughter*) Yes.
27. GARY: But it doesn't help.
28. SHARON: Not much.
29. BETTE: Well . . .
30. SHARON: No, but . . .

UNIT THREE

Monolog (SHARON)

I heard a story about a movie director who was making a movie a few years ago. And this guy had a . . . problem with English. He'd . . . would speak but often people couldn't understand what he was saying. He was almost incomprehensible.

Well, the movie company had spent lots and lots of money to make this movie. And the . . . and the, uh, sets were very expensive . . . hundreds and hundreds of dollars. And there was this one scene in the movie that the assistant director had decided to film in almost total darkness for a special effect. And the, the first, uh . . . movie director said, "No, no, that's terrible. I don't like that at all."

And the assistant director said, "But it's artistic, you know. It's very nice."

And finally the director shouted the man down and he said, "Eliminate it! Just eliminate it!"

Well, the sets were very elaborate, you know, and what can you do? Well, the next morning the director went to the movie studio and he looked around and he didn't see the set at all. And it was such an expensive set he couldn't figure it out. So he went and found the assistant director and he said, "Where is that set? It was a very expensive set."

And the assistant director said, "Well, you told me to eliminate it."

And the director said, "No, you idiot. I didn't say, 'Eliminate it,' I said, 'Illuminate it!' "

Discussion

1. GARY: If you had to choose, what kind of job would you, uh, uh, do?
2. CHUCK: I'd like to be a space pilot.
3. GARY: A space pilot!
4. SHARON: A space pilot?
5. GARY: Why?
6. BETTE: 'Cause he's spaced! (*laughter*)
7. CHUCK: That's right.
8. GARY: No, seriously . . .
9. CHUCK: Because I think it would really be exciting and it's new . . .
10. GARY: You're really serious?
11. CHUCK: I certainly am. Very serious. Yeah. That's true.
12. SHARON: Really? I never thought about it. I . . . I . . . mmm . . . I really like teaching.
13. BETTE: Just think of all that math you'd have to take.
14. GARY: You like teaching, Sharon.
15. SHARON: Mmm, very much. But . . .
16. CHUCK: Well, of course, I like teaching.
17. SHARON: But . . . I mean if I had to do any kind of job, I think teaching is really what I'd want to do.
18. CHUCK: But choose something besides teaching . . . what would you do?
19. GARY: Yeah, yeah. Choose something besides teaching.
20. SHARON: Mmm, if I chose something besides teaching . . .
21. BETTE: I'd be, uh, a violinist.
22. SHARON: Really?
23. BETTE: Or a concert pianist.
24. SHARON: Really?
25. BETTE: Yeah.
26. CHUCK: Really, Bette?
27. SHARON: Hmm.
28. CHUCK: Hmm.
29. GARY: The reason I asked is because I just don't have any idea of what I would want to be.
30. CHUCK: Aren't there things you'd like to be? Oh, I can think of ten things just . . .
31. BETTE: Oh, a dancer too . . .
32. CHUCK: . . . very quickly that I'd like to be.
33. BETTE: I'd love to be a dancer.
34. SHARON: Hah!
35. CHUCK: I'd like to be an anthropologist.
36. BETTE: Or an actor . . .
37. CHUCK: I'd like to be a writer.
38. BETTE: . . . uh, I mean an actress.
39. SHARON: Oh, that's what I'd like to do!
40. GARY: What?

41. SHARON: . . . you know, really. I would really like to be a writer.
42. CHUCK: What kind of things would you like to write?
43. GARY: Oh, that's hard work.
44. BETTE: A poet.
45. SHARON: Essays.
46. CHUCK: Essays?
47. SHARON: Mmm.
48. CHUCK: What kind of essays?
49. SHARON: I . . . I just like the whole idea of writing essays. You know, of . . . of really thinking about something and then writing . . . that way. Although I . . . I would also like to write short stories.
50. CHUCK: I like doing new things that haven't been done before. That's why I'd like to be a space pilot.
51. SHARON: Mmm.
52. GARY: That's been done before.
53. CHUCK: Well, yeah, mmm, every time they do it though, it's different.
54. BETTE: Not to Venus.
55. CHUCK: That's right or there's many places that . . . yeah. Oh, I'd really like to do it.
56. SHARON: Go ahead, Gary, think. What would you like to do?
57. GARY: Well, the reason why I asked all of you is because I have no idea. I wanted to get your opinions.

UNIT FOUR

Monolog (CHUCK)

When I was a little kid, I had a real thing for turtles. And one day I went into a pet shop, uh, to look for a turtle and they had a lot of different turtles in the pet shop.

And . . . there was one kind of turtle that I liked a lot. So I asked the shopkeeper, uh, inside the shop, uh, if those turtles were healthy. And he said, "Oh, yeah," that they were really healthy. And I said, "Well, uh, how long do you think this turtle will live?"

And he said, "Oh, it'll probably live at least ten thousand years and maybe even more."

Uh, and that made me really happy. So I told him okay, I'd take it. So he put it in a box and wrapped it and poked some holes in it so the turtle could get some air and I took it home.

And the next morning when I woke up, I wanted to go and play with my turtle. And I went in and looked in the turtle bowl, and the thing was dead already which really made me angry.

So I ran back to the pet shop and I said to the same clerk who was there, "That turtle you sold me yesterday's already dead."

Uh, and the shopkeeper said, "Really? Oh, that's too bad. I guess yesterday was its birthday and it just became ten thousand years old then."

Discussion

1. GARY: What do you all do when you're angry? Is there any special thing that you do?
2. BETTE: I take and throw dishes on the floor. And you know what's really awful is when the dishes don't break! (*laughter*)
3. GARY: You actually . . . you actually throw dishes on the floor?
4. SHARON: You really throw dishes on the floor?
5. BETTE: Yes, I get out these coffee mugs I've got and I just throw it as hard as I can.
6. SHARON: What are you going to do on your tatami floor?
7. BETTE: I don't know.
8. CHUCK: Wow, I don't want to be around you . . . yeah, I don't want to be around you when you get angry next time.
9. GARY: Really, I've never known anybody to do that . . . you see it in the mo- . . .
10. SHARON: What do you do, Gary?
11. GARY: Well, I usually don't talk.
12. SHARON: Really?
13. GARY: Yeah, I become very gloomy.
14. SHARON: I kind of do the same thing. I really get quiet.
15. CHUCK: I just like to be alone. I'd rather not be around anyone.

16. SHARON: My little sister used to throw shoes at people. (*laughter*) . . . Really! I can't tell you how many shoes I've had to duck.
17. BETTE: My mother would do that too, you know. One day she threw a shoe, uh, at my brother and it went right through the door. And she had to hide the hole in the door from my father. (*laughter*)
18. GARY: How long, Bette, have you been throwing dishes on the floor and where did you pick this up?
19. BETTE: Oh, well . . .
20. SHARON: From her mother.
21. BETTE: No, no . . . you know, sometimes you're in a situation where you get mad at somebody and they're not available so you can't tell them how mad you are.
22. GARY: Mmm . . . mmm . . . mmm . . .
23. BETTE: Um . . . so the next handiest thing is to take it out on the dishes and actually that's a better way of coping with it, you know, rather than getting into a row with someone.
24. SHARON: Maybe, but it doesn't really solve the problem if there's a problem.
25. BETTE: Well, sometimes, you know, you can understand a situation, but, uh, (*sigh*) . . . still be upset by it.
26. SHARON: I think so.

UNIT FIVE

Monolog (SHARON)

My sister Pam had a really beautiful figure when she was younger because, uh, she used to pay a lot of attention to the things she ate and she didn't eat a whole lot. And a couple of times she would enter, uh, local beauty contests and stuff, swimming suit stuff and she had really kind of a nice body. But she got married and she had a couple of kids and she's not quite as thin as she used to be. As a matter of fact, uh, sometimes she doesn't pay very much attention to the way she looks at all.

And we were talking the other day and she was telling me that when she first got married, the kids at the university next to her house used to really give her a hard time when she went out to . . . to sunbathe in the summertime. And they would whistle and yell and sometimes she really had to just go in the house. And she said, "You know, that really doesn't happen very often anymore. I really don't understand why."

And I looked at her and I said, "Really?"

Discussion

1. CHUCK: How do you feel about nudity in art? Does it bother you?
2. GARY: I'm for it.
3. CHUCK: Or do you have any special feeling or anything?
4. BETTE: Oh, I really like it. As a matter of fact, I'd like to experiment with taking artistic photographs . . . of, of nudes, nude males.
5. CHUCK: Really?
6. GARY: Really?
7. SHARON: I never thought about it a lot, you kn- . . . in my college it was quite a problem at one time. It . . .
8. CHUCK: Why would your college . . .
9. BETTE: You mean you had a lot of students running around nude? (*laughter*)
10. SHARON: No, but one of the artists on the, in the art department had done some, some paintings and he used his wife as a model. It disturbed a lot of people.
11. BETTE: Oh, well, you know though, that's, that, that's really very parochial thinking, because the n-, nude body is supposed to be the ultimate challenge to an artist . . .
12. SHARON: Well, I, I . . .
13. BETTE: . . . to be able to portray . . .
14. SHARON: Yeah.
15. BETTE: . . . meaningfully.
16. SHARON: I think so too, but I, I guess it depends on how it's done too.
17. CHUCK: Well, a few years ago I saw a very famous nude, uh, Goya's nude . . . a reclining lady.
18. SHARON: Did you, oh, did you see that here?
19. CHUCK: Yeah, one of the most beautiful paintings I've ever seen.
20. SHARON: Hah!

21. CHUCK: Uh, I don't see how any person could object to anything like that.
22. GARY: Do you ever feel strange, any of you, you know, looking at a, a nude painting or nude statue? Say, for example, you were in a big room someplace and there were a, there was a Greek . . . or Michelangelo statue . . .
23. BETTE: I feel, oh, I . . . I feel strange only in that, if it's something that's so incredibly beautiful and well done, it's very touching that, uh, somebody, to think that somebody could actually do that . . .
24. SHARON: Well, I . . .
25. CHUCK: But couldn't you feel that same way about any piece of art though?
26. BETTE: Oh, yeah . . .
27. CHUCK: Which means that you don't really overreact . . . yeah . . .
28. BETTE: . . . well, I don't make a distinction between nude and other kinds.
29. CHUCK: Yeah, that's good.

UNIT SIX

Monolog (SHARON)

Last winter we had kind of a, uh, cold winter and I was home in bed reading one night and listening to my radio. And, uh, the disc jockey who . . . was kind of an interesting guy who would . . . he would play records and talk to his radio audience, uh, announced that it was, uh, about eight degrees outside the radio station.

And then he went on to say that he was a little curious about the temperature in the rest of the city and if people were up, why didn't they check their temperature and . . . call in to the station, tell him how cold it was where they lived, and then he would announce it to everybody else listening to his program.

And . . . well, I was sort of comfortable so I didn't get up, but I . . . kept listening to the radio station and couple of minutes later somebody called in and it was a kind of funny little old lady. We could hear her voice, of course, over the station.

And she said, "Well, I checked my temperature and it's normal just like always . . . ninety-eight point six."

Discussion

1. BETTE: You know, I feel really dumb. Um, there's so much that I don't know and so much happening and so much to read that I . . . I can't process all the information available. Do y'all feel the same way?
2. GARY: I . . . I know . . . yeah, I know what you mean . . . There, there's so much to find out about in so many different ways nowadays. We have television, we have radio, we have all sorts of magazines.
3. SHARON: Even in your own field, you know, you'd have to read twenty or thirty magazines a month in order to keep up.
4. CHUCK: Just to know what's happening, that's right.
5. SHARON: Yeah.
6. CHUCK: And especially so when you consider the whole world.
7. BETTE: Yeah, that's the thing. You know, now, whereas before, our sphere of interest was maybe just our country or our area, because of communications systems, uh, your sphere of interest is the whole world.
8. CHUCK: Yeah, yeah, that's right.
9. GARY: And before, people didn't realize that they sh-, I . . . I think we realize now that we should know things. And therefore, we are pressed to know these things . . .
10. BETTE: Well, we're . . .
11. GARY: . . . whereas people before didn't understand that.
12. CHUCK: But, I think, uh, it's physically impossible, uh, to keep up with everything that's going on all the time. And I think in our own adjustment we've got to realize that, that we just can't do it. And then work from there . . . somehow.
13. SHARON: But at the same time you feel that way, you think that as a . . . educated adult, you have to keep up with . . . with certain international events and affairs or else not really be a responsible person.
14. BETTE: Yeah . . . yeah, you know that, that's it . . . it's your responsibility in making decisions about not only your own life, but, you know, uh, other things, contributing in some way and you have to be informed to be able to do that.

15. GARY: You have to learn to pick and choose information too.
16. BETTE: Yeah.
17. SHARON: Or read faster. (*laughter*)
18. CHUCK: Yeah, that's a good point though, picking and choosing information, like . . . and being able to depend on the sources of your information.
19. SHARON: Really.

UNIT SEVEN

Monolog (GARY)

Little Timmy's only seven years old and he comes from a big family. He's got six brothers and sisters. Being the youngest, he's always had to put up with taking hand-me-down clothes and waiting until the bowls at the dinner table get to him last and really having to share everything. Uh, finally, after sharing most everything including clothes and even a room, he got his own room. But it didn't last very long because his mother became pregnant again. So his father thought that he would sit down with Timmy and have a heart-to-heart talk and his father asked him, "Timmy, which would you prefer, another brother or another sister?"

And Timmy said, "Well, if it's all right with you and Mom, how about just a pony?"

Discussion

1. BETTE: You know, I used to have this boyfriend who was so stingy that he bought me paper flowers 'cause they would last longer. (*laughter*)
2. SHARON: Really?
3. CHUCK: Well, that's a good idea.
4. GARY: That's pretty stingy. That's pretty stingy. When you receive a gift like that, apparently you were affected by it, you would have felt better, wouldn't you, had you received, uh, real flowers?
5. BETTE: Well, roses, of course.
6. SHARON: Did you think it was funny at the time?
7. BETTE: Well, I did because this person was so stingy that even for him to buy paper flowers (*laughter*) was being generous for him. (*laughter*)
8. SHARON: Oh, Lord. You know, my . . . some sisters and brothers have grown up since I've known them and I was very interested to hear my mother talking about how stingy one of my sisters is who used to be very generous. I think it's very interesting.
9. CHUCK: Mmm . . . mmm . . .
10. BETTE: I wonder what makes people stingy.
11. GARY: Well, maybe it's a confusion of terms. A person, I think, can be stingy. Then a person can be thrifty. And so many times those two terms are, uh . . .
12. BETTE: Yeah.
13. GARY: . . . confused.
14. BETTE: And a person can be poor too.
15. GARY: And poor.
16. CHUCK: Yeah, yeah, but sometimes the . . . the person's a combination of those two, I feel.
17. SHARON: Stingy and poor, or stingy and thrifty?
18. CHUCK: Stingy and thrifty.
19. GARY: Give an example.
20. CHUCK: Give an example?
21. GARY: Mmm-hmm. You mean, uh, like a person has money and, uh, he wants to buy something and maybe he doesn't buy it because he's saving his money for . . .
22. BETTE: Or he buys for himself, but he doesn't buy for others.
23. GARY: Oh, now that's stingy.
24. BETTE: Yeah, well . . .
25. CHUCK: Yeah, that's definitely stingy.
26. GARY: That's not thrifty. That's stingy.

UNIT EIGHT

Monolog (SHARON)

I was working as a legal clerk in Judge Brown's office for a long time and a rather funny thing happened one day. Uh, one of the policemen who worked in, uh, the town came in to the judge and said, "Judge, you know, there's a car parked in a no-parking zone and it belongs to a rather important person. What do you think I should do?"

And the judge said, "Well, the law's the law. If it's in a no-parking zone, surely you have to tow it away."

So the policeman left and I guess he towed it away. Little while later Judge Brown went out for lunch and he came back and he said, "Where's my car?"

And I said, "Well, I don't know," and, uh, just then the policeman came back and, uh, the policeman said, "Are you looking for your car?"

And Judge Brown said, "Yeah, wh-, where is it?"

And he said, the policeman said, "Well, it was your car that was in the no-parking zone. I'm very sorry."

Discussion

1. GARY: You know, the other day I went to a drugstore trying to find medicine that I needed for a cold and the . . . the druggist wouldn't sell it to me.
2. SHARON: Really?
3. GARY: Yeah.
4. SHARON: Didn't he have it?
5. GARY: Yeah, he had it. And it was the kind of medicine I had bought before but, uh, apparently now you have to have a prescription from the doctor to buy it.
6. CHUCK: But I think that's good . . . because I think often people depend on . . . medicines too much when they could get by without taking stuff.
7. GARY: Mmm . . .
8. BETTE: Well, I know, but, uh, (*sigh*) you know, I don't really think you should have laws against any kind of a drug. I think the choice should be up to the individual. And if a person is really a hypochondriac, it doesn't make any difference whether you have to have a doctor's prescription or not.
9. SHARON: Really?
10. BETTE: Sure.
11. SHARON: But if you don't know what it is and you can go in and buy anything, don't you think there would be some trouble?
12. BETTE: I don't think so. I mean, people don't know what they take now, even with a doctor's prescription.
13. CHUCK: Well, I agree with you that . . . the laws certainly should be freer about drugs, but I do feel that there're some drugs . . . and medicinal things . . . I'm thinking of now, like, for example, that medicine that Gary was talking about that I do think ought to be sort of controlled.
14. GARY: Sure, uh, the antibiotic drugs, in general, if you take a lot of them, after a while your system becomes immune to all helps that the drugs can give you. That's why there's a prescription needed.
15. SHARON: But I thi-. . .
16. CHUCK: Sharon, you told me recently about somebody who took an overdose of vitamin C. People are taking a lot of vitamin C and he took too much. That could happen to anybody. Didn't you tell me that?
17. SHARON: Yeah, it could happen to anybody, of course.
18. BETTE: But you know what . . .
19. SHARON: I think maybe I agree with Bette though, I mean, why should there be a law against drugs?
20. CHUCK: You mean drugs of any kind.

UNIT NINE

Monolog (CHUCK)

My cousin Steve was six years old when he got his own room. Since the birth of a younger sister, he'd been sharing a room with her. At school he heard from some of his friends that they all had their own rooms. Naturally, after hearing this he decided that he, too, wanted his own room.

Uh, he began telling his mother and father as often as possible that he wanted a final- wanted a private room.

Finally his father gave in. There was an extra room in their house that they'd been using as a kind of catchall storage room. They cleaned out that room and fixed it up and finally told Steve that it was his. Steve was really happy. He made all kinds of rash promises that he never kept, uh, especially about keeping it clean.

On the first night it . . . that he slept in his new room, there was a terrible thunderstorm. It was the first thunderstorm that Steve had ever experienced. It was just awful. Lightning was flashing and the thunder was so loud that the house seemed to be shaking.

After a few minutes, Steve's parents went to his room. They thought he'd be scared to death in all that noise.

But Steve wasn't scared at all. He was just mad. He was so mad his face was red. He said, "Now I understand why you gave me this room. It's so noisy here that no one else wanted it!"

Discussion

1. SHARON: Did you have your own room when you were little, Gary?
2. GARY: No, for I think the first twenty years of my life, I had somebody else in the room with me.
3. SHARON: What about you, Bette?
4. BETTE: I didn't when I was very little . . . uh, up in a . . .
5. SHARON: Yeah, and Chuck, you did because you didn't have any brothers and sisters.
6. CHUCK: I've always had my own room.
7. SHARON: I always wanted my own room, you know, because there were seven of us in the family and we always had to double up and stuff. Maybe, I had my . . . my own room the first time when I was about twenty-five or something.
8. GARY: I was very happy when my sister got married because then I could take her room.
9. SHARON: Oh, really?
10. GARY: And for the first time I had my own room, I felt very proud.
11. SHARON: Yeah.
12. BETTE: I did too. When I was . . . started to go to high school, my parents thought it was time that I had my own room.
13. SHARON: I wish my parents had thought that, but there were only four bedrooms in our house for nine people so we really were . . .
14. CHUCK: So I'm the only one here that's really had his own room all his life . . . but I have . . . but I don't know . . .
15. BETTE: What do you think that's done for you?
16. CHUCK: I think it's . . . I think it's generally good. I think whenever possible because I think it makes people feel more independent and maybe a . . .
17. BETTE: Well, do you think even a small child should have their own room?
18. SHARON: I think so.
19. CHUCK: Sure, sure.
20. BETTE: Mmm, I don't know. What age?
21. SHARON: I really do. I . . . I think from the beginning.
22. CHUCK: Yeah, I think so too.
23. BETTE: No, I don't.
24. SHARON: Why?
25. BETTE: Well, I think, uh, I think, uh, for like a small baby, you know, until you're maybe at least a year or two years old, uh, just the sense of security that develops in a child in . . . in the presence of other people, you know, and if a child's just put in a room . . .
26. SHARON: Mmm . . .
27. CHUCK: But . . .
28. BETTE: . . . in a cold room with . . .
29. CHUCK: I don't mean just put a child in a cold room and ignore him.
30. SHARON: I think you probably should do that.
31. GARY: Ignore the child? (*laughter*)
32. SHARON: No, I'm just joking, of course.

UNIT TEN

Monolog (GARY)

The stewardess had a hectic time on a trip from one coast to the other. Uh, sh—. . . . there were lots of air pockets and the plane kept going up and down and with all the passengers filling the plane, uh, and trying to serve them food and drink, it was just a real bad time for her. To compou-. . . uh, to make matters worse, uh, there were lots of passengers who were complaining, asking for blankets and glasses of water and aspirin and magazines and the poor stewardess was just totally exhausted. Well, making matters even worse, was this kid running up and down the aisle shouting and hitting people and making all sorts of noise. And at one point he even, uh, uh, knocked the stewardess almost into the lap of a, a sleeping gentleman. Well, when this happened, she bent down after spending a long, hard trip and she smiled sweetly and whispered in the child's ear, "Little boy, why don't you go and play outside?"

Discussion

1. BETTE: Sharon, do you like to fly?
2. SHARON: Mm, very much. It's really exciting every time I get in an airplane.
3. BETTE: Have you ever thought . . . have any of you ever thought about, uh, taking flying lessons?
4. SHARON: Uh-huh. I'd like to, actually.
5. CHUCK: So would I, very much.
6. GARY: Not me.
7. CHUCK: Really?
8. GARY: Every time I get on a plane my . . . the palms of my hands start to perspire.
9. CHUCK: Oh, I like flying.
10. BETTE: I do too, Gary, but . . .
11. CHUCK: Really, Bette?
12. BETTE: . . . uh, I took flying lessons myself . . .
13. SHARON: Did you really?
14. BETTE: . . . simply because I was so . . .
15. SHARON: When?
16. BETTE: . . . terrified. Um, the last, well, maybe about two years ago I took a ground . . . ground pilot. And then I have a lot of friends who fly.
17. CHUCK: How many hours was that . . . of instruction?
18. BETTE: Well, ground pilot is like, is only, I don't know, it's a semester. It was an evening course at the university, huh? To prepare you for your written exam. And then I have a lot of friends who fly small planes, so . . .
19. CHUCK: Did you ever fly?
20. BETTE: Yeah. But you know, with an experienced pilot in the seat.
21. GARY: Did you overcome your fear of heights in flying?
22. BETTE: Oh, nooo. It was even worse because I knew . . . (*laughter*) I knew just enough to . . . to, uh, get frightened but not to know exactly what to do, you know, and one time . . .
23. SHARON: Mm.
24. BETTE: . . . we were flying into Kaanapali.
25. SHARON: Hah.
26. BETTE: And the plane . . . we made about six approaches. And everybody was out on the runway taking bets on whether we were going to land or not. I was terrified! I was really terrified.
27. CHUCK: Did you land?
28. BETTE: Yes, we did. (*laughter*)
29. GARY: Whenever I go on a long, long trip by plane, I take sleeping pills so I'll sleep.
30. SHARON: Oh, Gary, but . . . you miss all the fun.
31. CHUCK: Yeah, that's what I think, Sharon, 'cause I really like . . .
32. SHARON: You know, every time the plane taxis and the minute it leaves the ground, I think it's like a miracle.
33. CHUCK: Yeah.
34. SHARON: I mean, I, my, my, my whole body is just filled with joy.
35. GARY: I think it's like a miracle and I don't believe it's going to make it. (*laughter*) That's why I take sleeping pills.
36. SHARON: Oh, I love it.
37. BETTE: Oh, it's also, too . . . especially in a small plane, you're really close to nature.

UNIT ELEVEN

Monolog (SHARON)

A lot of people travel to foreign countries in the summertime and it's really a good experience. I've done a lot of that myself and I've seen a lot of interesting things when I've traveled.

One time I was sitting in a restaurant watching the people come in and out, just drinking some coffee, and kind of enjoying the experience of being in another place. I watched at one point two people come in and sit down at a table. They didn't quite know what to order and they didn't speak the language at all, but there were pictures in the menu and they thought, well, they could probably get by just pointing at things so they pointed at something and the waiter seemed to think that was reasonable because he didn't ask any questions. So he brought what they were supposed to eat. In doing so, he brought the sauce for the meat that they were going to eat first and put it on the table. The two people who were eating didn't understand what they'd ordered so they didn't know what he'd brought. They looked at it and since it was in a small bowl, they thought, "Well, this must be the soup," and they drank it. You can imagine their surprise to find out that it was almost a hundred percent vinegar!

Discussion

1. GARY: You know, the other day af–. . . after Chuck left, I looked and the space underneath the table where he was sitting eating breakfast and I found some coffee stains. So, I wiped them up and, uh, then, the next morning . . .
2. BETTE: You found some more. (*laughter*)
3. GARY: In the very same place.
4. SHARON: Really?
5. GARY: Yeah.
6. CHUCK: Well, what's wrong with that? I enjoy my coffee. If I spill a little bit, . . .
7. GARY: It's crazy. I, I, I, I have this thing about a clean place, you know.
8. SHARON: Have you always been like that, Gary?
9. BETTE: Very fastidious.
10. GARY: Not . . . not . . .
11. SHARON: You know, when I was in college, I hardly ever made my bed or cleaned my room. I really didn't at all . . .
12. GARY: Uh-huh.
13. SHARON: . . . and my first roommate in Honolulu . . . I never cleaned the apartment and now I really every day make my bed, every day clean the room and every day keep things neat.
14. CHUCK: Sharon, do you do it because you want to or because you feel you ought to?
15. BETTE: Is it a compulsion?
16. SHARON: No, because . . . no, because I really want to.
17. CHUCK: Really?
18. SHARON: Yeah. But I think it's become kind of habit too.
19. CHUCK: I don't think it's so important if you're comfortable. I don't think it makes so much difference.
20. BETTE: That's true. That's true.
21. SHARON: It depends on how many other people you affect.
22. CHUCK: Well . . . of course.
23. GARY: It depends on what kind of animal you are, you know. It's like a pig. Living with a pig.
24. BETTE: Oh, it is not, Gary!
25. SHARON: No, Gary. Not really.
26. CHUCK: Oh, Gary.
27. BETTE: It's not, Gary. It's just that somebody . . . I . . . I am at sometimes compulsively, neurotically . . . ah, uh, you know . . .
28. GARY: Yeah. (*laughter*)
29. BETTE: . . . in a clean . . .
30. GARY: You want to clean things.
31. BETTE: Housecleaning! Yeah, I just have to.
32. GARY: Yeah. Yeah. Yeah . . . I feel the same way.
33. CHUCK: Fortunately, I never feel that way.
34. BETTE: And sometimes . . . sometimes . . .
35. SHARON: Unfortunately, you never feel that way. (*laughter*)
36. CHUCK: But I just don't think it's so important. Sometimes, maybe.

37. BETTE: That's true. There're a lot more important things to do.
38. CHUCK: Mmm.

UNIT TWELVE

Monolog (CHUCK)

My cousin Steve has never been what you would call a good student. The family tells a story about Steve when he was, uh, in grade school. Uh, at that time the teachers encouraged the students to read a lot and tried to always get them to learn to use new words. Sometimes the teachers were successful and sometimes they weren't. Often with Steve they weren't.

One day in class they were giving reports from newspapers. One student read to the class about a politician who was very good with, uh, anecdotes.

Steve didn't understand the meaning of *anecdote,* so he asked the student, "What does *anecdote* mean?"

The student, who was probably, uh, very happy to show off, told Steve that it meant "story" or "tale."

Of course the teacher was listening and she told Steve to try to make a sentence with *anecdote* in it. Steve thought and thought, but he didn't say anything.

The teacher said, "Oh, Steve, that's easy. You just heard that an anecdote is a tale."

Finally Steve said, "Last spring my dog Spot had three puppies. After a few days my dad cut off all their anecdotes."

Discussion

1. BETTE: What do you folks think of sending three-year-olds to nursery school?
2. SHARON: I think it's kind of a good idea. Tamon's little girl goes to nursery school, and she likes it very much.
3. BETTE: Why do you think it's a good idea?
4. SHARON: Because she's an only child at the moment and her mother has to take care of her and she enjoys being around other people her age, I mean, little kids.
5. GARY: I think it depends on what the child learns in the nursery school. What sort of thing are you talking about, Bette? What kind . . .
6. BETTE: I was thinking of a fairly formal thing, you know, like the Head Start programs where you're training a person to go into kindergarten or the first grade.
7. GARY: Well, teaching them what? Reading?
8. BETTE: Yeah, yeah, not just a play situation.
9. CHUCK: I think it depends very much on that family's situation and that particular child.
10. SHARON: Yeah, I think so. And I think even if it's not a play situation, it's not a bad thing.
11. CHUCK: Mmm, by play situation, you . . .
12. BETTE: You don't think that maybe you start structuring a person, you know, too much, too soon? I mean, I think our educational system is very structured and very repressive . . . you're just starting the process a couple of years earlier if you . . .
13. SHARON: Well, if it's more of the same thing, I agree, I think.
14. CHUCK: But, Bette, wouldn't it be possible, uh, to sort of start some sort of creative thing earlier? Would you be in favor of that?
15. GARY: You mean like art? And things like that?
16. SHARON: Mmm, even like reading is creative . . .
17. CHUCK: Well, Bette says that education is . . . is repressive and I agree and I'm wondering if it could be not repressive earlier.
18. BETTE: Well, I'm also thinking, too, about what age a child starts to socialize and I don't think they're ready for socializing outside of the family, you know, before the age of about five or six.
19. GARY: Yeah, I agree with you.
20. CHUCK: Oh, really?
21. GARY: There are other ways of socializing, uh . . . uh, with other children than sending your child off to a nursery school.